Tell Me I Can't...
and I Will.

DANIEL G. HORGAN

ACKNOWLEDGMENTS

This book was inspired by my late grandmother, Marie A. Walters, and is dedicated to my family and Mike who have shown me unconditional love. I am super grateful for my team of editors including mom, dad, Tom, Bill, Dan, Kyle, Amy, Steve, Jeffrey, Amy, Jackie, and Holly.

ISBN: 1502827484
ISBN-13: 978-1502827487

CONTENTS

Introduction   1

1   Let Your Legacy Guide You   3

2   Align You with You   10

3   Be Restlessly Energetic   17

4   Carpe Diem – Seize Each Day With Passion   23

5   Train the Voice Within   30

6   Curate Inspiration   38

7   Tell Great Stories   43

8   Build Championship Teams   50

9   Manage People, Not Widgets   57

10   Empathize   65

11   Go to the Front Line   74

12   Influence Change   80

13   Jog and Sprint   86

14   Charge Through with Optimism   90

15   Don't Burn Out   96

16   Be Relevant   102

17   Never Stop Discovering   108

18   Stay in the Arena   114

My Closing Wish   120

INTRODUCTION

"If you can't fly then run,
if you can't run then walk,
if you can't walk then crawl,
but whatever you do
you have to keep moving forward."
-Dr. Martin Luther King Jr.

Have you ever reached a breaking point -- a moment when there is an energy that crashes through your mind and your body like a wave in a restless sea? You fight for the strength to retreat but instead the world witnesses you, uncensored. Your words and actions come gushing out, fueled by the desire to be heard, to be seen, and to be understood. You either spread rage like a wild fire engulfing anyone and anything in your path or unknowingly commit, in a moment, to being authentic. In either case, you release yourself into the wild. You break free from the cage that you have settled within. Each bar represents a voice of discouragement; each lock is reinforced by the excuses that you have made. You spread your wings; you ruffle your feathers. You break your silence and release a passion for change. Your breaking point is a moment of restlessness where you no longer find comfort in excuses. You find freedom in your voice and actions.

You are restless for change. You want no more excuses. You are begging for authenticity. You are searching desperately for a platform on which you can stand with pride. You are yearning for acceptance and a commitment to embrace your diversity of thought, DNA, and dreams. Self-help books, motivational speakers, and the change agents that have come before you have fed you a vision of possibility leaving you hungry with hope.

It is your time to not back down but instead to stand up and speak out. Being silent is no longer an option. Complaints without solutions are like a poison that satisfies your needs in the moment but leaves you craving more, an addiction to negativity that will not seed change. If change is what you are after, then you must spark a movement in your mind that is energized by your heart and soul. Let your restlessness give breath to your body from your fingertips to your toes, sparking movement that tackles one step at a time.

Stand still and you will go nowhere. Dream small and you will delay giving yourself what is rightfully yours to seize. Close your eyes and envision your success. Focus on the feeling of pride that you have when celebrating victory, when overcoming adversity and proving naysayers wrong when they doubt your potential. Commit yourself to change and to decisions aligned with your vision.

We are at a breaking point...no more excuses...be restless. Tell me I can't...and I will.

Chapter 1: Let Your Legacy Guide You

"Everyone has his own specific vocation or mission in life; everyone must carry out a concrete assignment that demands fulfillment. Therein he cannot be replaced, nor can his life be repeated, thus, everyone's task is unique as his specific opportunity to implement it."

-Viktor Frankl

It was my freshman year in college. I was working three jobs, maintaining a 4.0, and hearing all about how my friends from high school were building new relationships, selecting study abroad programs and choosing which fraternities and sororities they were going to pledge. I couldn't help but reflect on my own life, challenging myself to answer what seemed like a daunting question: what am I doing with my life?

What appears to be a moment of self-pity was actually a turning point in my life. It was through this period of self-reflection that I taught myself a powerful life lesson. **Life is what you make it.** Your end game, your legacy, is a compilation of the choices you make and the subsequent consequences of those choices. You must lead your movement in life.

I remember closing my world history book and driving to Barnes & Noble to peruse the self-help section. I scoured the shelves in search of a coach, someone that could inspire me, push me, teach me, and open a world of possibilities that I couldn't see at the moment. After reading countless book jackets, I came across a book on tape series from Zig Ziglar called Goals: Setting and Achieving Them on Schedule. Since my commute to school and work was about 45 minutes each way, I settled on the idea of turning my car into a laboratory, a place where I could invest in me without feeling judged, criticized or mocked. I could experiment with new ideas, answer difficult questions, and struggle to articulate my goals, my vision, and my purpose. It was my safe zone, and Zig was my coach. Together we shared many commutes, several ah-ha moments, and a lot of growth.

Zig coached me, "If you can dream it, then you can achieve it." He went on to say, "It was character that got us out of bed, commitment that moved us into action, and discipline that enabled us to follow through."

I hung on every word that Zig shared. I dissected it. I wrote in my journal about it. I spoke his words out loud. I started to believe it.

Equipped with Zig's lessons in mind, I set out on a journey that I continue to embark on today. I have soaked in the words of Stephen Covey and Marcus Buckingham along with Spencer Johnson and Malcolm Gladwell. I have internalized 7 Habits and put my Strengths to Work. I have embraced the Outliers and discovered Who Moved My Cheese? I have taken risks, made difficult decisions, and relied on my faith in myself to leap forward. Although there have been critics and judgments along the way, they are muffled by the sound of my persistence and diluted by the purity of my purpose.

I seek to change the world by equipping, elevating and evolving others. This is the legacy that I aspire to contribute to each day and ultimately leave behind. I build this legacy by sculpting my words and actions to inspire and by feeding those that are hungry for change and thirsty for hope with confidence. I walk hand in hand with the oppressed whose attitudes prevent them from imagining, discovering, seeking, and achieving their purpose. I coach. I listen. I embrace and acknowledge.

I am not perfect. I evolve with each person I meet, each experience I encounter, and each risk I take. And while it may feel as though there is an abundance of problems and a scarcity of solutions along the journey, I reflect on Zig's wisdom, "Building a better you is the first step to building a better America."

The journey to sculpting a personal legacy requires a great deal of self-reflection and vision. It does not happen overnight. In fact, you strengthen and create your legacy over the course of your lifetime. It is intricately tied to your values and in your control. If someone were to strip away all of your material possessions, financial resources, and relationships, you would still be in possession of your vision. It is locked away in your mind and serves as an internal compass, your own personal guide in life.

Imagine an artist at work in her studio about to create a piece of pottery. She envisions a beautiful vase modeled after an ancient Roman urn she saw recently on an exhibit at a local art museum. With her vision in mind, she goes to work with just the clay, a potter's wheel and her hands. The artist explores the piece, alternating leadership roles with the clay. Sometimes she follows the natural movement of the clay on the wheel allowing nature to unfold in her hands. In other moments, she takes the lead with her fingers shaping and pinching the clay. The clay collapses on the wheel. She starts again recalling her original vision. After multiple attempts, the clay and her vision align and a masterpiece is sculpted.

Just as an artist sculpts a clay masterpiece, we create a vision in our minds of what we want to create in our lifetime. We define the legacy that we wish to be remembered by someday. Through both leading and following along our way, each step may not be exactly what we anticipated or set out to accomplish. However, the end game, our desired legacy, is where our focus must not falter. The path to our personal legacy may present some unexpected turbulence and a few wrong turns, but a commitment to utilizing our internal compass will eventually steer us back on track.

Motivational speaker Tony Robbins coaches us, "Progress equals happiness." **The reality is that we are going to make mistakes and bad decisions in life, but as long as we are making progress towards creating and strengthening our legacy, we will be happy.**

If you think about it, we have encountered legacy questions dating all the way back to elementary school when we were asked, "What do you want to be when you grow up?" We have forced students at a younger age to pick career paths as they pursue enrollment in choice, charter or magnet schools. College entrance and scholarship applications have challenged us to define our goals in life. Job interviews and career coaches often pose the question, "Where do you see yourself in 5, 10, or 15 years from now?"

Stephen Covey conveys the importance of visioning in his book, The 7 Habits of Highly Effective People, with the second habit, "Begin with the end in mind." Covey writes, "Habit 2 is based on imagination – the ability to envision in your mind what you cannot at present see with your eyes. It is based on the principle that all things are created twice. There is a mental (first) creation, and a physical (second) creation. The physical creation follows the mental, just as a building follows a blueprint."

Consider how coaches train their teams to envision a series of plays on the field prior to the actual game. Watch Olympic athletes before they compete. They are playing out their moves in their minds. In the production of any movie or television show, all of the writers, producers, directors, set designers and lighting professionals are creating a vision in their minds that they collaborate on and bring to life on the set. Teachers prepare lesson plans with learning objectives in mind. Lawyers anticipate a jury's response to their closing arguments with a desire to appeal to their emotions and logic.

No one has a magic ball that they can look into and see how their future will unfold. We do, however, have the ability to shape our future by defining our desired legacy. With a clear vision in our minds, we make more thoughtful decisions each day about the experiences we engage in and the relationships that we invest in. With each decision, we focus on the legacy that we are trying to create and utilize our vision like a filter. Our legacy filter is much like a personal coach that doesn't judge us but guides us by putting our vision in front of us like a reflection in a mirror.

I think that defining our legacy is like putting together a giant jigsaw puzzle. The first step is to spend some time analyzing what the completed puzzle will look like, the vision that is necessary to make sense of all of the individual puzzle pieces. The image of the completed puzzle is an analogy for your life which is comprised of hundreds of experiences, personal interactions, various jobs, and all of the challenges and celebrations that have unfolded in your life, each of which represents a piece of the puzzle.

Some pieces are going to be more important to you like corner pieces. Consider the corner pieces as representing the people and experiences in your life that have served as an anchor for you, that have contributed to the defining moments in your life in which you achieved a goal or lived out your values.

In the end, our jigsaw puzzle illustrates one story represented by a collection of pieces that were assembled with hard work, determination, luck and vision. **The legacy that we strive to create and be remembered by should represent a vision of a life well lived with purpose and passion. It should showcase how we have realized our full potential across the unique dimensions of our lives, delivering impact that only we could advance.**

Take Action: Let Your Legacy Guide You

- Inspired by Jack Nicholson's 2007 movie, "The Bucket List," develop your own bucket list of activities that you want to accomplish in your lifetime. Include places you want to travel to, experiences that you want to have, people that you want to reconnect with or meet, books that you want to read (or write), awards that you are striving to achieve, etc.

- Create a vision board using words and images cut out of newspapers and magazines that represent the goals that you plan on achieving in your lifetime. Reflect on similar items as those outlined in the bucket list activity above. Place your vision board somewhere that you will frequently view it as a reminder of all that you hope to accomplish.

- Consider the tagline that would summarize how you would like to be remembered someday. These taglines often center us and aid us in defining our desired legacy. For example, you may want to be remembered as "a selfless mother" or "a tireless advocate for human rights." Create a nameplate for your home or work desk including your tagline.

Chapter 2: Align You with You

"People will forget what you said, people will forget what you did, but people will never forget how you made them feel."

-Maya Angelou

Take out a piece of paper, and make a list of the brands that surround you. Think about the clothes that you are wearing, ads that pop up online, billboards you pass by, mail you receive and commercials on TV.

Once you have generated a healthy list of 18-24 brands, circle the ones that most resonate with you. The brands that you circle should foster a connection with you that relates to your life experiences, values, and interests.

Next to each of the brands that you have circled, jot down how you view the brand. For example, is the brand hip, trendy, and smart? Does the brand make you laugh or appeal to your emotions? Can the brand help your performance by fueling your body or challenging your mental state? Does the brand spark a bond with you and win your loyalty?

The brands that surround us are more than eye catching logos and memorable jingles or taglines. They don't exist to just compete for our time and attention in an over-saturated sea of other brands. Brands tell a story behind products and services. They encapsulate and define an experience that is carefully crafted to attract and engage you. Equipped with research on targeted demographics, brands are designed to capture our imaginations, relate to our life experiences, and connect with our dreams and aspirations. Successful brands speak to their targeted consumers in relevant tones, words and imagery.

Heidi Cohen of Riverside Marketing Strategies wrote, "A brand creates perceived value for consumers through its personality in a way that makes it stand out from other similar products." **In the same way that businesses of all sizes develop, advance and evolve their brands, each of us has a personal brand that we project through our words and actions.** There is an experience that people have when they interact with us that relates to our personality, work ethic, and decisions.

To identify your personal brand, reflect on the feedback that people have provided you either casually or through more formal channels such as performance reviews or 360 feedback activities. What kind of friend have you been to others? Are you known for being a great listener, or have you been valued for giving great advice? Do you motivate your friends and inspire them through your own perseverance? What is typically noted on your performance reviews at work? What role do you tend to play on teams? Do you assume leadership or prefer to follow? Do you hang out in the background or actively contribute? Are you positive and optimistic, or are you known as the naysayer or devil's advocate?

Another way to gather insight on your personal brand is to simply ask people directly. Ask friends, family members and colleagues at work to share adjectives that come to mind when thinking about you. Inquire about what your blind spots are and where they see you holding yourself back.

Gathering input from others is important because sometimes the perceptions that we have of ourselves are not aligned with how others would describe our personal brands. If this is the case, we have some work to do, and that work requires a commitment to self-reflection and honesty with ourselves.

Through the years, the gathering of feedback from others along with my own self-reflection has opened my eyes to areas in which I need to improve as well as areas in which I excel. Comments that I have received regarding my public speaking skills have fueled my passion for training and development and given me the motivation and courage to continually refine my skills in this area. 360 feedback gathered from individuals that I have managed has helped me to evolve into the manager that I am today. I have always been hungry for feedback. Even when what I hear is not positive, I view this constructive feedback as an opportunity to gather additional perspectives and to evaluate how my actions and words influence others.

An executive coach once challenged me to view my weaknesses as overextended strengths. For example, my focus on producing high quality work is a strength and often desired on the job and while working with teams. When my focus on quality is overextended to the point that I am consistently pushing for perfection, I can turn people off and hold up a project. Hearing this feedback is not easy, but when I reflect on it further, it is incredibly helpful to be more self-aware in future collaborations and to apply this lesson to other aspects of my life.

Often times, we think that our personal brand is a list of all of our accomplishments. While our resume certainly contributes to our personal brand, it does not define our brand in its entirety. As Forbes contributor, Glenn Llopis, wrote, **"Your personal brand should represent the value you are able to consistently deliver to those whom you are serving."** That means that regardless of whether you are writing a blog, collaborating on a project at work, or serving on a nonprofit board, your personal brand is in play and those around you are assessing the value that you are contributing.

Many times, we look up to others as role models and leaders that we wish to emulate. It is easy to fall victim to the practice of following their every move and replicating their actions as though they were our own. Even worse is when we hang on every word that they speak and blindly agree with their opinions to stroke their egos. If you think that this adds value, consider the words of personal branding expert, Dan Schawbel, "Be the real you because everyone else is taken and replicas don't sell for as much." **Part of defining our personal brand requires us getting comfortable in our own skin and mind so that we are looking internally to reveal the skills and strengths that we uniquely possess.** These are our tickets to success and will shape an authentic personal brand.

There are three key reasons why I believe so much in the power of personal branding.

1) **Defining our personal brand requires a continual commitment to reflecting on how we are adding value to the environment and people around us.** Strengthening our self-awareness muscles consistently reminds us to be present. When engaging with people, we are not glued to our phones or drifting off in our minds to contemplate what is next in our schedule. Rather, we are present with people, listening to their words, reading their body language and considering if and how we can add value. This level of presence is noticed more and more today given all of the distractions that surround us. Our presence builds trust and cultivates relationships over time. When we are fully present, we do not miss opportunities that surface.

2) **Evolving our personal brand challenges us to engage ourselves within self-appointed stretch assignments.** These assignments can test our assumptions, aid us in developing new skills, or help us to further refine our strengths. They push us beyond the boundaries of our comfort zone and diversify our influence and impact. For example, if we know that we are uncomfortable in networking situations, we can craft a challenge for ourselves to reposition the situation as an opportunity to add value, to demonstrate our personal brand in action. We are not being called on to simply schmooze and socialize. Rather, we have an assignment to add value to someone in need.

3) **Our personal brands are closely tied to the legacy we are striving to build and leave behind one day.** The value that we have added to people's lives or in organizations where we have been employed lives on beyond our direct interactions. Think about the letters of recommendation that you have received or the testimonials that clients have shared with you. Your personal brand is not based on a single experience. It is based on a collection of experiences that are interwoven over time to define your value, to tell your story. Therefore, how you bring your personal brand to life each day and evolve it over your lifetime shapes what people recall about your values, contributions and impact. How you are remembered someday will be rooted in the perspective and attitude you adopt, the

words and actions that you deploy, and the commitment and impact that you advance.

Ultimately your personal brand is yours to define. Make people's experience with your brand memorable. Add value.

Take Action: Align You with You

- Maintain a compliment log in which you keep record of the compliments that you receive from colleagues at work, friends, and family members. Overtime, you will begin to see trends surface across the compliments that you have received. For example, you may notice that many people highlight your artistic skills or your ability to listen actively and give great advice.

- Regardless of whether you are seeking a new job or admission into a post-secondary degree program, gather recommendations from mentors, coaches, teachers and colleagues. Review the recommendations gathered over time and call out the trends highlighted from diverse sources. This is great information to leverage in shaping and evaluating your personal brand.

- Brainstorm at least 24 words that relate to the personal brand that you would like to bring to life through your words and actions. Assemble these words into a word cloud, enlarging those words that most align with the brand that you want to represent. The word cloud can serve as a visual reminder in your home or at work representing how you want to be branded and as a decision making tool.

Chapter 3: Be Restlessly Energetic

"What helps luck is a habit of watching for opportunities,
of having a patient but restless mind, of sacrificing one's ease or vanity,
or uniting a love of detail to foresight, and
of passing through hard times bravely and cheerfully."

-Victor Cherbuliez

Have you ever found yourself so preoccupied by a particular task or challenge that you completely lost track of time? Your determination remained steadfast from start to finish. Even in those moments when you thought you couldn't make it, you pushed through and convinced yourself otherwise with an adrenaline that fueled your commitment. When you crossed the finish line in achieving the task or overcoming the challenge, there was an abundance of joy released inside of you. You smiled, clapped and internally told yourself, "way to go." With a jolt of energy, you wanted to tell the world, shout from mountaintops that you did it and showcase what you accomplished.

In those moments of great personal satisfaction and accomplishment, we discover the zeal inside of us. Zeal is defined as an "eager desire" and an "enthusiastic diligence." It is that surge of energy that propels us along, intensifies our commitment, and carries us across the finish line to victory. The zeal that we possess has no limitations except for those that we self-impose. In some cases our zealous nature is in direct conflict with the internal voice inside our heads. We may waver between the courage and tenacity to succeed and the defeatist attitude convincing ourselves that we should give up.

Our zeal is like a muscle that we must build, massage and test. The challenges that surface in our lives can create the playing field upon which we call our zeal into action. When we do not like something, we should examine whether it is within our control to change it. If our minds and actions can advance a solution, we should deploy them with great zeal. Keep our focus in the game and pursue each play as if it were the most critical to our victory. And when we get tackled or knocked off our game, we should jump up, dust ourselves off and get back to work. Recall the words of Frederick Douglass, "If there is no struggle, there is no progress." People will not often hand us the ball, the tools to employ in our game of life. We will need to remain diligent in our search for opportunities, seize them when they surface, and celebrate our progress along the way.

I often reflect on The Serenity Prayer that my parents shared with me at a young age and reference it often when I am faced with a big decision or a challenge that seems insurmountable. "God, grant me the serenity to accept the things I cannot change, the courage to change the things I can, and the wisdom to know the difference." If we try to change those things outside of our control with zeal, we most likely will reach a state of anger, frustration and cynicism that will blind us from the opportunities that arise in what we can influence and control.

We must learn to identify the priorities in our life and direct our attention, commitment and zeal to those efforts. Theologian John Wesley preached, "Do all the good you can, in all the ways you can, to all the souls you can, in every place you can, at all the times you can, with all the zeal you can, as long as ever you can." These positive investments of our time and talent will create returns that hold greater value than any monetary allocation.

Even when we encounter people that try to sideline us from our passion and dreams, we must leverage our zeal to push onwards. Some will try to persuade us that our goals are impossible and that the challenges we seek to address are insurmountable. Their words will call to question our ability to influence change. While some find comfort in hardship out of fearing the unknown, others live with a mental state of depleting hope. Their trust of change has been tested too often and unfortunately their experience has convinced them that change is a lie. These people may have heard of Mahatma Gandhi's words, "You must be the change you wish to see in the world," but their attempts to change have failed. As a result, they despise change and thrive in routine.

Throughout my life, I have identified these people as a source of motivation. I acknowledge their beliefs and experiences while striving to prove them wrong. My efforts are not fueled by a desire to position myself as better than anyone else. Rather, my restless commitment to change is rooted in a strong desire to be a beacon of inspiration, a spark that tests assumptions and elevates people's potential. I draw on

George Bernard Shaw's advice, "When people shake their heads because we are living in a restless age, ask them how they would like to live in a stationary one and do without change." **Despite what people may project on the surface with their words, internally people are hungry for change but unsure how to proceed.**

I am sure that each of us has encountered a challenge that we knew was important to address but we did not have a roadmap to guide us step by step in addressing the challenge. We may have contemplated a whole series of moves before ever taking the first step. Then something or someone served as the catalyst that got us moving. We took one step at a time. Sometimes we stumbled and fell backwards two steps. In other cases, we sprinted ahead as though the path before us was clear of all hurdles.

English philanthropist and politician Charles Buxton believed that "experience shows that success is due less to ability than to zeal." I believe that zeal, above the skills or tools and resources that we may have available, is what matters most in our quest for change. Our zeal relates to our attitude, and as life coach Zig Ziglar always promoted, "It is not our aptitude, but your attitude, that determines your altitude." We can soar to new heights with an attitude that believes in our own potential. **With zeal, we will stay the course and remain restless until our vision morphs into reality.**

When I was in college, I launched a nonprofit organization that offered a summer program for kids in an under-resourced neighborhood. In designing the program, I engaged a team of staff members that felt the same level of urgency to meet the kids' needs. At the same time, we were aware that these kids were confronted with so many more challenges in their lives that we did not understand nor did we have the resources or knowledge to resolve. None of us had ever created a summer program from scratch, but with a great deal of zeal, we learned to thrive in a state of ambiguity. We outlined the program's core elements and sought to engage the kids themselves in shaping the rest. Our transparency with the kids won us respect and engaged them at a level that they had never experienced before. The program surpassed everyone's expectations and taught the kids more than we had ever set out to deliver. They learned so much about leadership, goal setting, civic engagement, communications and conflict resolution...all skills that equipped them for their life's journey.

We must keep in mind that our zealous commitment to fulfilling our dreams requires the collection and use of knowledge and data along the way. Scientist Thomas Henry Huxley calls out that "zeal without knowledge is fire without light." We can be fired up about an issue or an injustice, but facts and data to support our case will build the credibility we need to gain momentum. **Knowledge equips us with power while zeal provides us with energy and feeds our passion.** In combination, knowledge and zeal win respect. Respect mobilizes followers by persuading people to believe. Followers validate our commitment, surface synergistic ideas, and spark a viral campaign of advocates. In the process, our fire serves as light and change is inevitable.

Now regardless of whether you are seeking to influence a project at work, pull off an effective charitable fundraiser or spark a movement for a social justice issue, zeal is an essential tool in your toolbox. A laissez faire approach in projects that you care about highlights a lack of urgency, delays change, and demonstrates a commitment to status quo.

I urge you to be restless and embark upon a prioritized set of projects with zeal. Define your commitment with the attitude you deploy and turn on the light that you were born to shine.

Take Action: Be Restlessly Energetic

- Keep a log of the activities and tasks where you notice yourself losing track of time and showing up with greater energy and enthusiasm. Pay attention to your body language, too. You will notice when you are leaning in more, sitting up straight, and feeling a burst of energy through your body. These are instances where your zeal has surfaced!

- Take the ambiguity challenge. Get involved in a project that engages people you don't know or pushes you outside of your comfort zone. For example, volunteer at a senior center or with children in an after school program. Sign up to teach a computer literacy course for immigrants or offer to conduct mock interviews for veterans. When we practice working in an ambiguous situations where we have little experience, we can discover a lot about ourselves and make connections that we wouldn't otherwise have made.

Chapter 4: Carpe Diem - Seize Each Day with Passion!

"Everything can be taken from a man but one thing:
the last of human freedoms – to choose one's attitude
in any given set of circumstances, to choose one's own way."

-Viktor Frankl

What lights your fire? What gets you out of bed in the morning? What puts a smile on your face while filling your mind with inspiration and ideas? What propels you to take action? What hits you at your core? What makes you sit up and come alive in your body language? What do you lose yourself in? What makes your heart beat faster and your mind race?

Passion breathes optimism into our attitude and sustains our energy. It motivates us to take action and risks. It serves as a catalyst for achieving our dreams and shaping our legacies. The autobiographies of successful leaders and entrepreneurs often identify passion and their conviction to a positive attitude as part of their success story.

Consider for example the passion that Abraham Lincoln exuded over the course of his adult life. Lincoln failed to get elected to public office 5 times before he was elected President of the United States at the age of 52. His passion for serving his country was unwavering; his attitude won him respect. Walt Disney's passion for imagination and creativity was unyielding and fueled his career in animation and his vision for the Disney theme parks. Disney used his passion to alter the attitudes of those that experienced his work by shifting their mindsets from what **is** to what **can be**. Bill Gates's passion for software and innovation made him a trailblazing businessman and continue to inspire his philanthropic endeavors. His attitude is exemplified by the words Microsoft once used, "Change the world or go home."

All around us are examples of people living passionately with inspiring attitudes. Teachers are selflessly giving up their planning periods or lunch breaks to tutor students. Doctors are volunteering their time in local health clinics to care for the uninsured. Lawyers are taking on pro bono cases for women in shelters struggling to escape abusive relationships and rebuild their lives. College graduates are committing to a year or two of service through AmeriCorps or Peace Corps programs which strive to reform our education system, to construct homes for the homeless or to establish clean water sources in remote, third world villages. People of all ages and backgrounds wake up each morning with a fire in their belly. Their attitude propels them out of bed, into action and on a path to delivering results. Their passion fuels and sustains their commitment over time and through obstacles.

Some people, however, have not yet discovered, embraced and advanced their passion. Their attitudes are sour, and their optimism has eroded. They struck out too many times, convinced themselves that change is unlikely, and breed negativity through their words and actions. Somehow their fire has grown weak and they have committed to just surviving, existing day to day. Unfortunately I have seen this lack of direction, purpose and energy in youth and adults alike across rich and poor neighborhoods where hope has been depleted, dignity discarded and dreams deemed impossible. Apathy consumes these individuals blinding them to their own potential.

I, myself, have experienced times when I woke up each morning for weeks or months to relive the routine that I lived the day before, moving throughout my day like a zombie caught in a funk. I moved in the direction that I was told and accepted the world as it unfolded without questioning the circumstances. I ate, worked, and slept...over and over and over again. I lived each day without purpose or direction. Somehow I lost my way.

Then there is that defining moment when we change our attitude. Something inspires us, it compels us to action. We change the internal dialogue in our head from "I can't" to "I will." We commit ourselves to action, and we take the first step. One by one, we cut the strings of our puppeteer and our new attitude, our fresh outlook on what we can accomplish, gives us the strength to move on our own. We take ownership of our decisions. We find our voice. We heed the advice of Henry David Thoreau, **"Go confidently in the direction of your dreams. Live the life you have imagined."**

As a child, I can recall playing school quietly in my room, dreaming of what it would be like to be a teacher. I took old worksheets and pretended to grade papers with a red marker using stickers from my collection when the assignments were done exceptionally well. I hung sheets of paper on the wall as my chalk board and pretended to teach lessons by writing out math problems. My imagination soared as I dreamed of one day standing in front of a classroom inspiring my students to work hard, give their best effort and achieve great things...all lessons that my parents had taught me.

I went confidently in the direction of my dream, and as a student of my own experiences, I began to conclude that my dreams were not enough. No matter how hard I tried, there were obstacles beyond my comprehension and ability to resolve. I met students who were so abused that each night they considered taking their own lives to escape into their dreams where they were safe. I worked with single parents who worked three jobs to provide a roof over their children's heads, food on the table, and clean clothes on their backs, all while subscribing to the belief that one day the American Dream would be realized. I met donors and politicians who were so far removed from the front lines of poverty that their actions put band aids on problems and photos in papers with captions selling dreams. I encountered compassionate volunteers who made commitments that were underappreciated. Over time, they became discouraged and their dreams wilted, too.

I used to believe that dreams alone could drive change. Then I realized that the first two words in Thoreau's quote above are the most critical, "Go confidently..." I began to understand more with experience, with each interaction and relationship that I fostered, that **the act of movement and the spirit of confidence are what give breath to our dreams, a heartbeat to our imaginations.**

Each year we welcome in the New Year by setting resolutions and sparking new dreams. Most of us will put forward a strong effort and launch into pursuing our goals. Many of us will hit a wall, become discouraged, make excuses and shy away from our resolutions. Our new dreams will retreat into the back of our minds and be remembered during those "what if" moments in our lives. We repeat the same process each year, hoping that one year will be different. We anticipate the year when we have the confidence to take a journey marked by countless steps and the courage to stay the course.

Thoreau writes, "As a single footstep will not make a path on earth, so a single thought will not make a pathway in the mind. To make a deep physical path, we walk again and again. To make a deep mental path, we must think over and over the kinds of thoughts we wish to dominate our lives."

Thoreau's words remind me of a character in my favorite movie, "Dead Poets Society," in which Robin Williams plays Mr. Keating, an English professor at a private boarding school. Keating yearns to inspire, to teach and to challenge his students to "go confidently" in pursuit of their dreams while learning from the legacies of those that have come before them. Mr. Keating instructs his students to examine archived pictures of students who have graduated earlier, to look into their eyes and recognize the similarities to themselves. Mr. Keating reminds his students that they share those same dreams, fears and invincible feelings. He then whispers the words "carpe diem, seize the day" and challenges his students to live the legacy of those before them in order to make their lives extraordinary.

Each of us has the opportunity and the ability to seize the day, to make our own lives extraordinary. Our dreams create an inspiring starting point. They can pull us out of our static lives, jump start us on a pathway to our destiny, and challenge us to realize our potential. Our commitment to movement and our spirit of confidence will keep us on track, help us to avoid the pitfalls and potholes along our journey, and maximize our potential. Our confidence will give us the strength to endure moments of defeat and words of criticism. Our movement will enlighten us with experience and introduce us to characters whose stories will inspire and shape our perspective, values and decisions.

I ask for you to join me in this movement that refuses to accept a defeatist attitude. Curate experiences, words, and actions that inspire people to acknowledge the control that they have on their attitude.

Seek to be the spark which lights the fire in someone's belly. Live a life of example so that you can prove what is possible when you discover, embrace and evolve your passion each day. Be a beacon of hope that guides people to the defining moment where their attitude shifts and they commit to re-engaging the magic of **their** character. The choice is ours to make, and our attitude will determine the results.

Listen to the words of educator, author, and civil rights leader Howard Thurman, **"Don't ask yourself what the world needs. Ask yourself what makes you come alive, and go do that, because what the world needs is people who have come alive."** Let passion breathe life into your mind, heart and soul so that you can cross the finish line, achieving what you set out to accomplish. With passion and a winning attitude, we do not just **walk** that line. We **sprint** to the end with gusto, having led a life of true happiness and fulfillment.

"There is one quality that one must possess to win, and that is definiteness of purpose, the knowledge of what one wants, and a burning desire to possess it," writes Napoleon Hill. **Your passion is your gift to the world.** Your attitude determines whether you will deny the world the passion you were born to deliver or seize the day.

Carpe diem, my friends! Carpe diem!

Take Action: Carpe Diem – Seize Each Day with Passion

- Watch "Dead Poets Society," and pay attention to how Mr. Keating challenges his students to discover and embrace their passion in life.

- Create a daily to do list. Don't let a day pass you by without taking charge of how you spend your time. Reflect on your to do list often throughout the day to maintain focus and revisit the to do list at night to celebrate what you accomplished. Reflect on why you were unable to achieve some tasks and start the next day reinvigorated and with a clear focus on your priorities.

- Align with the 80/20 rule by inventorying how you are currently spending your time. Code each task on your inventory with an "A" for aligned or a "NA" for not aligned with your personal passion in life. The reality is that we all have tasks in our lives that we are not super excited about completing. A good goal to focus on is aligning at least 80% of your activities with your passion. The more that you are aligned, the more energy you will feel and the greater contribution you will make.

Chapter 5: Train the Voice Within

"Sometimes I lie awake at night, and ask,
'Where have I gone wrong?'
Then a voice says to me,
'This is going to take more than one night.'"

-Charles Schulz

There is a voice inside our heads that has the ability to propel us forward or hold us back. Sometimes this voice is one of reason, providing direction in moments where we need a guide in life. Yet, at other times, this voice is a bully, punching us in the gut while trying to convince us that our potential is limited and our talent is weak. **The voice inside our heads is one that we must train and control for our confidence, success and significance depend on it.**

Think about the last time when you were about to enter an uncomfortable situation. Perhaps you were attending a high school reunion, getting ready to take the stage for an important speech, or hosting a critical business meeting. Do you recall what the voice inside your head was saying to you? Was it giving you a coach's pep talk before the game, firing you up to tackle the play that lay ahead of you? Or was it chiseling away at your confidence, causing you to question your ability to be successful? All of us have most likely encountered both voices at various volumes and frequencies in our lives. Regardless of what the voice is saying to us, the real test that we face is what we do after hearing it. It is the attitude that we adopt in those critical moments that defines the influence of our internal voice and the actions that we pursue.

I remember when I was 18 years old and working to launch a nonprofit organization in Pittsburgh that would serve as the local affiliate to the national America's Promise movement, launched by retired General Colin Powell in 1998. The mission of the organization was to provide kids with five promises including a caring adult, a safe place, a healthy start, an effective education and opportunities to serve. I had been fortunate to have all of these promises in my life and was determined to ensure that kids in Pittsburgh and beyond had them as well. What I didn't anticipate was the reaction that I initially received upon trying to spark the movement in Pittsburgh. Several foundations and businesses told me that I was too young and that while my efforts were to be applauded, I should seek the guidance and direction of someone more experienced to lead the way.

For a brief moment, I let their voice persuade the voice inside of my head. I kept hearing over and over again, "You can't do this." I took control of the voice inside my head, fighting back with gusto, and turned their words of discouragement into a challenge that I would whole-heartedly accept over the next seven and a half years while leading Allegheny County's Promise. I surrounded myself with people of all ages that believed in me, fueled my passion, and partnered with me to fulfill our mission for hundreds of kids. I did not return to the naysayers in spite but rather with results in hand and proof of what a "kid" could lead. I gained their respect, and in many cases, I altered the voice inside of their heads.

Our model in Allegheny County was the first youth-led Promise effort which landed me an invitation to join the national board of directors, which was comprised of national celebrities, CEOs of Fortune 500 companies, respected experts in the youth development field, and well-respected community activists. I remember attending my first board meeting with a lump in my throat and butterflies swirling about in my stomach. I must have tied my tie a thousand times while getting dressed and rehearsing in the mirror what I would say to people when I was introduced. But when my big moment came, I simply said "thank you for having me" and remained silent the rest of the meeting. My silence was sustained for several meetings as I soaked the experience in, observed everyone's movements, and hung on every word that they spoke. The voice inside my head that had once played "you can't do this" on replay had a comeback. I wanted desperately to silence that voice and gain the courage to speak up, but the intimidation and fear of being judged for my opinions kept me silent.

It was not until about a year later that I found myself in a coffee shop after one of the board meetings with some senior leaders from the organization and a few board members that I started to control my inner voice and realize that my voice at the table had a purpose. We were brainstorming strategy on the back of napkins and placemats like grassroots community organizers. Despite the significant difference in our experience levels, our perspectives were all equal and respected. I had come to life in that collaboration energized by the team asking for my insight and compelled to contribute because of the impact that we could have in advancing our mission. It dawned on me at that moment that I was there to represent all of the communities that were striving to deliver the promises for kids just like mine. I had an obligation to demonstrate the importance and value of having youth represented in the movement.

We all struggle at times with finding and using our voice. I have learned that the more I focus on training my voice by adopting the right attitude, the more often my voice is a tool in my toolbox that I leverage to move me closer to my goals and aspirations. Steve Jobs of Apple once advised, "Your time is limited, so don't waste it living someone else's life. Don't be trapped by dogma – which is living with the results of other people's thinking. Don't let the noise of others' opinions drown out your inner voice. And most important, have the courage to follow your heart and intuition." **Silencing your voice does no one any good.** It withholds your perspective from the world which could spark others' ideas or generate a solution. It depletes your confidence and limits your ability to fully live a life of purpose.

One of the tips that I often share with people on training their inner voice is to identify a personal theme song. Although it sounds silly, picking a theme song that you play in your head before you tackle a challenging play builds up your energy, confidence, and determination to use your voice. It gets your blood flowing while your body and mind get into gear. Two of my personal favorites are Frank Sinatra's "That's Life" and Sam Cooke's "A Change is Gonna Come." They both inspire me and remind me that what may seem like an improbable hurdle today could be the victory we celebrate tomorrow. If I am really in need of a spike in my confidence or the energy to get moving, I will rely on R. Kelly's "The World's Greatest" and Technotronic's "Pump Up the Jam." Laugh if you must, but stop and consider which songs really inspire you and energize you to take action.

Vincent Van Gogh once wrote, "If you hear a voice within you say 'you cannot paint,' then by all means paint, and that voice will be silenced." Sometimes our inner voice can be pretty persistent at holding us back, so in those cases, I encourage you to push onward and commit to working hard at proving yourself wrong.

Also, remember that just like you have an internal voice sometimes working with you and sometimes against you, those around you have an internal voice in their heads as well. **Consider how your actions and words can be the catalyst for them conquering their internal fears and self-doubts.** If we are reminded that our internal voice can be combatted with the right attitude and that someone is cheering us on, that can make all the difference in terms of how we show up, speak up, and stand up for change.

The following is a poem that I wrote to articulate the frustration that we sometimes feel when others limit our potential, when their words or actions demonstrate a disbelief in our ability to be significant in a world that demotivates so many. We question our purpose when we lose hope, and one of the hardest choices that we make is to stand out, to speak up, and to be honest with ourselves…to be significant.

Insignificant Me

Me? Insignificant?
Insignificant me.

I've allowed you to define me.
The adjectives you use place me in a box
so that your joy grows and my confidence wilts.
The glare in your eyes strikes me
with a cold breeze of hostility…jealousy…anger.
I yearn for compassion
but feel invisible in your presence.
You work the room around me.
You speak words that cause me
to question my very existence…my purpose.

I take one step forward...
proud of what I have accomplished
and yet you mock me. You push me down.

I want to stand tall.
I want my voice to echo loudly.
I want people to hear what is on my mind...
to see what is in my dreams.
I want to take people on magical adventures
through my imagination and
breathe hope into a world of despair...pain...
sorrow breeds in your rejection.

Insignificant me.
I don't blame you.
I stand in awe of you.
I silently watch your moves...patiently follow your direction.
I wonder if what you show the world
is rooted deep within an insignificance that *you* fear.
But the moment that I get too close you shut me out.
You put me in my place...my place of insignificance.
Suddenly everything that I believed crumbles
and I am left picking up the pieces of a puzzle
that seems impossible to mend.

I get defensive.
I get angry.
I throw my hands in the air and I scream...
who are you to define me?
What gives you the right to shape my destiny?
Why have I allowed myself to stumble
into the palm of your hand only to be suffocated
and tossed aside as though I never breathed a breath.
You did not hurt me.
Your words did not break me.
I broke myself the moment I let you into my head.
I let your words eat away at my soul,
and I let your character trump my offer to this world.
The second that I questioned my potential
may have been your victory...but I let you win.

I was in control.
I am in control.
I define me...my purpose...my existence.
I define my destiny with the choices that I make...
with the actions that I take.
You make me stronger.
You push me to my limits and challenge my values.
The only way that I am insignificant
is if I define myself that way.

I am significant.
I have a purpose.
I add value.
I have a voice that deserves to be heard
and a mind that will not be limited.

Significant...that's me.

Take Action: Train the Voice Within

- Identify your theme song (or songs). Think of songs that have lyrics that motivate you or a beat that gets you moving and feeling pumped up. Play these theme songs before making a presentation or when you feel as though you need a jolt of energy. You'll be surprised how quickly your mood and confidence change.

- Play a word game with yourself where you swap out all of the negative or self-defeating words in your vocabulary with more inspiring or action-oriented words. For example, swap out the phrase "I can't" with "I will give it a try." Instead of "problems," focus instead on "opportunities."

- To support others in their quest to train their internal voice and to give ourselves some positive energy, accept the compliment challenge. Throughout your day, look for opportunities to share genuine compliments with co-workers, friends, neighbors, and family members.

Chapter 6: Curate Inspiration

"The best and more beautiful things in the world cannot be seen or even touched- they must be felt with the heart."

-Helen Keller

Have you ever witnessed a special moment that causes you to smile on the inside and out? It is like a flash in time where for a few seconds everything around you freezes. You hone in on an act of kindness that comes to life before your eyes. The characters of the act have chosen to share compassion and humbly do so without seeking recognition. In fact, when the kindness is acknowledged, a rush of embarrassment surfaces and the character retreats into saying, "it was nothing." But it was something; it was a special moment of inspiration.

I once witnessed a colleague who arrived early to the office prepare a hot cup of coffee with all the fixings for the woman that cleaned our floor. As the woman got off the elevator and started making her way down the hallway with her cart full of cleaning supplies, my colleague jumped up and with a big smile handed the woman the coffee with a warm "good morning." The smile emanating from that woman's face has been permanently implanted in my mind. I recall that smile in moments when I am searching for inspiration.

There was another moment when I was driving through a neighborhood in DC and stopped at a traffic light. I witnessed a homeless man with a plastic grocery bag picking up trash in a public park. When his bag was full, he unloaded it in a garbage bin and continued picking up more trash. The homeless man is someone's son, perhaps someone's brother or father. And while most people pass him by without acknowledging his existence, he finds a purpose for his life and seeks no recognition.

I was at a coffee shop once when a young girl in front of me offered to help an elderly man who was having trouble seeing and counting his dollar bills. When she realized that his coffee was $2.15 and he only had a $1 bill, she paid the balance with a smile and wished the man a nice day.

In the flurry of activity that consumes each day, I have challenged myself to focus on noticing the special moments that are playing out all around me and to spark special moments myself. In doing so, I have recognized a difference in my attitude and a stronger yearning to share compassion. Simply smiling at someone on the elevator or in the hallway can sadly be the only smile or acknowledgement that someone gets throughout their entire day. Telling someone how much they are valued or acknowledging the extra effort that they put into a project is a simple task for us to do. Yet sometimes we neglect such simple actions in order to get on with life and of course the next project. We fail to be a beacon of inspiration.

Regardless of how successful someone is or how many possessions that they obtain, people are in search of something more meaningful. There is a hunger among people for hope and inspiration. They want to be moved, to feel something. In a world full of demands on people's time, we all want the world to pause for a second so that we can be reminded of what really matters. Sometimes we want the chance to breathe so that we can see and acknowledge people and feel inspired.

We get so caught up in the hustle and bustle of our daily routines that we grow blind to the special moments unfolding all around us. We grow cynical when someone offers to help, thinking that they are motivated to get something in return. The media scares us with their stories of scams and profiles of people on the hunt to hurt. There is a scarcity of stories depicting agents of change or servant leaders that selflessly commit themselves to causes that meet people's needs, build community, and advance justice.

We extend so much effort trying to be perfect that we forget that we are human. **There is a connection that all humans desire with one another. That is the need to feel accepted and a sense of belonging.** Fake friendships and politically-motivated relationships dominate our attention at times as we seek promotions and approvals. Our authenticity diminishes while conformity dominates our neighborhoods, schools, and workplaces. When someone is courageous enough to stand out and inspire us, that person reminds us that acceptance and belonging are not born out of uniformity. Rather, inspiration breeds acceptance. **When we trail blaze with inspirational acts, we give others permission and the motivation to do the same, to be the creators of special moments.**

Spiritual leader Marianne Williamson teaches, "Our deepest fear is not that we are inadequate. Our deepest fear is that we are powerful beyond measure. It is our light, not our darkness that most frightens us." **Each of us must address our fear of being powerful by continually**

nourishing ourselves with inspiration. There are countless fiction and non-fiction books that can serve as sources of inspiration. Through personal coaches and relationships with role models and mentors, we can gain greater inspiration from their advice and example. By creating an inspiration board of quotes, pictures and memorabilia that we see every day, we can remind ourselves how influential inspiration and special moments are in our lives.

There are two key lessons to remember when considering inspiration. First, **we all need inspiration in order to thrive.** We can go about our routines and become complacent in an effort to conform. But this practice will only enable us to survive. To thrive in life, we must draw upon those special moments that inspire us and feed our heart and soul. They will compel us to take risks, remind us to be authentic, and empower us to dream.

Second, **we all can be a source of inspiration.** Through our actions and words every day, in small and in large ways, each of us has the ability to spark hope in someone's life. By acknowledging people, genuinely caring for them, and being present with them, they will experience acceptance and be inspired to embrace their potential. Our individual inspiration can be a rallying call, a "pay it forward" challenge, to those around us to spread compassion and remind people how powerful they are.

So hit the pause button in your life. Look around you and witness a special moment. Take the time to find inspiration, embrace it, leverage it and call upon it often. Live an inspired life while inspiring others.

Take Action: Curate Inspiration

- Create a bulletin board in your home or office full of inspirational quotes, pictures and words. Leverage the bulletin board at least once a day to get some inspiration and remind yourself of how you can inspire others. Let the bulletin board be a living piece of artwork; continually add to it and change it so that it evolves with you as you learn and grow.

- Seek out at least 1-2 inspirational mentors and grab coffee with them once a month. Share stories from your lives, gather advice, share perspectives, and seek to inspire one another.

- "Pay it forward" at least once a week where you intentionally seek out opportunities to do something nice for a colleague, friend, family member or neighbor. Reflect on the feelings that you have after paying it forward.

Chapter 7: Tell Great Stories

"Great stories happen to those that can tell them."

-Ira Glass

Flash back to first grade. The school bell rings. The librarian gathers the attention of 30 kids rummaging for their carpet squares. We anxiously want to travel into space, step onto a pirate ship, or immerse ourselves in a mystery.

A hush falls over the classroom as the book cover is rotated for all to see. Colorful imagery draws us in and confirms that we are in for a treat as the librarian opens the book and turns to the first page. We hang onto her every word as she introduces us to the characters. She effortlessly flows from page to page drawing us further and further into the story. We reach the climax and feel as though we are right there with our new friends, faced with some overwhelming challenge. As we cheer them on in our minds, anticipating how they will get out of their predicament, the librarian closes the book and smiles.

We desperately want more. We want to finish our adventure. Instead, the librarian encourages us to use our imaginations. She asks us how we think the story will end. She probes and questions why. Then she wraps up story time by reminding us that we can check the book out at the public library.

These sessions always ended the same way. The librarian caught our attention every time. We were so excited to meet new characters and join them on their adventures which transformed us out of our realities and into a fictional world. The librarian reminded us every month that if we wanted to know how the story ended, we would need to take action.

I did not realize it at the time, but these childhood story times provided me with the first glimpse of how our lives unfold. There are chapters full of characters, dilemmas and conflicts, solutions and discoveries. Each decision we make has consequences and those consequences shape our lives. **We can use our imaginations and take action in defining the legacy we write as the author of our life. Or we can allow others to dictate our journey, to define who we are and what we stand for in life.**

The reality is that our lives are a series of stories that are born in our experiences and relationships, shaped through a process of internalization and woven together over time. Stories have the power to inspire us and discourage us. They can transform our opinions, values and sense of self-worth. Our life purpose and passion can surface through stories, and stories can transport us anywhere our minds are willing to venture. Stories are powerful, and the individual who can effectively compose and deliver a story adds value to this world beyond his realization.

Effective storytellers instantly capture our attention. They lure us into their story by appealing to our senses, breathing life into our imaginations, and sparking our recollection of experiences and characters in our own lives that relate to their story. There is a moment where their story transforms itself into our story as we internalize and personalize the words. This transformation is the measure of a storyteller's success and enhances the longevity and value of their story.

Think about masterful storytellers that you have encountered. Perhaps they keynoted a conference you attended, wrote a book you recently read, or deliver blog posts into your inbox each day. Maybe you tuned into one of their TED Talks, enrolled in one of their classes, or were fortunate enough to be managed by one. Regardless of where your paths crossed, you remember them and draw upon their stories. They brought their art to life by connecting with you personally regardless of how many others were present with you. **A powerhouse storyteller delivers stories in a brief moment of time that live indefinitely in the minds of listeners and can be shared exponentially around the globe and across generations.**

Annette Simmons, author of The Story Factor, writes, "A story gives people enough space to think for themselves. A story develops and grows in the mind of your listener. If it is a good story, you don't have to keep it alive by yourself. It is automatically retold or replayed in the minds of your listeners." From childhood fables to ghost stories and Shakespeare's poetry, stories have existed for centuries and can survive beyond the original storyteller. Artists, writers, orators, poets, actors and business leaders breathe life into their stories. New meaning is applied to stories over time as cultures evolve, people interpret the words in the context of their own lives, and pop culture principles are applied.

I believe that a critical step to becoming a storyteller that inspires people and drives impact in our organizations, communities and world is to listen to the stories that people are sharing around us. Former Secretary of State Dean Rusk advises, "The best way to persuade people is with your ears – by listening to them." **People are sharing their own stories every day in the decisions that they make, the comments that they provide and from the internal voice in their heads which propels them forward or holds them back.** They are showcasing their values, spotlighting their fears, and highlighting their dreams. If we listen closely and observe their actions, we will discover key messages that, if incorporated into our stories, would resonate with them.

If we learn to craft the stories that we share based on the trends that we discover by listening to and observing more intently the people and environment around us, our stories will project more meaning and connect more deeply with our listeners. **The authenticity we apply to our storytelling is equally as critical to the messages being shared.** While our stories are a reflection of the people and environment around us, they should also be a reflection of us. "Stories are how we think. They are how we make meaning of life...Stories are how we explain how things work, how we make decisions, how we justify our decisions, how we persuade others, how we understand our place in the world, create our identities, and define and teach social values," shares Dr. Pamela Rutledge, Director of the Media Psychology Research Center.

One of the most powerful leadership development programs that I participated in featured a seminar on leadership presence. The instructors were actors from New York City, and they facilitated a series of acting and improvisation exercises that pushed everyone in the class out of their comfort zones. Each of us had to recall a childhood memory that we acted out as a monologue. We were then tasked with identifying a life lesson we gained in that memory and crafting our monologue into a storytelling experience that we would share with our teams in our department. Our acting debuts featured many takes, lots of coaching, and constructive feedback from our peers.

The experience taught me that I didn't need a stage and microphone to tell a story. I could incorporate stories into my everyday interactions with my team members and managers to share context, persuade, inspire, and humanize myself as a leader in their eyes. I discovered that stories could foster greater connections with my colleagues that resulted in greater loyalty, cooperation, engagement, and ultimately results. John Kotter, Harvard Business School professor and author of Leading Change, writes, **"Over the years I have become convinced that we learn best – and change – from hearing stories that strike a chord within us...those in leadership positions who fail to grasp or use the power of stories risk failure for their companies and for themselves."**

One easy way to jumpstart your storytelling adventure is to brainstorm a list of defining moments in your life. Define what each of these moments has meant to you. What did you learn from the experience and the relationships involved? How did the experience inspire you to think differently or take action? How has the experience shaped who you are today? How do you believe that these "defining moment" experiences relate to the experiences that others have encountered? What lessons from your experiences would be relevant for others?

Pick one of the defining moments on your list and write your story out with a clearly defined, singular theme. Properly introduce and bring the characters to life in your story. Focus on appealing to all senses as you unfold the plot, and speak to people's hearts and minds. Keep your story simple and relevant to your targeted audience.

Now this may feel silly, but act your story out. Stand in front of a mirror or record yourself delivering the story. You could even practice with supportive and honest family or friends. Get familiar with your lines, internalize them and relive the moment through your words. Pay particular attention to your body language. Your facial expressions, hand gestures, and body movements all can breathe life into your story or suck the energy from the room. For your practice runs, overemphasize your movements and exaggerate your expressions and gestures. When it is time to perform, you will find yourself retreating back towards your comfort zone so your practice runs will stretch your boundaries and enhance your performance.

And yes, **storytelling is a performance**. At first it will feel uncomfortable and awkward, but in time, with more practice, it will feel more natural. The connections you make with people, the actions that you inspire, and the feedback you gather will propel you into believing in the power of storytelling. **Your stories have the power to take root in people's minds, sprout inspiration and action, and bloom further as your audience passes on your stories adding the context of their own lives.**

I'm listening...what story are you ready to share?

Take Action: Tell Great Stories

- Identify the defining moments in your life thus far that have played a major role in defining who you are today.

- Develop a personal story journal that is organized by categories. Consider which of your own stories address topics that may surface at work, with friends, or with family. For example, can you recall a story where despite putting your whole heart into a project, the outcome was not successful? Or perhaps you can think of a story where your perseverance paid off in the end.

- Capture and record the stories shared by others that impact you. Chances are these stories will impact others in your life as well.

Chapter 8: Build Championship Teams

"It takes two flints to make a fire."

-Louisa May Alcott

The setting is a school playground on a warm, breezy spring day. The recess bell rings and the kids stampede through the double doors pounding the pavement like the bulls in Spain. Some sprint to the swings, slides and sandbox while others dash over to the netted bag full of balls, bats and bases. Pickup games of baseball and kickball take off and teams emerge.

The kids naturally take on roles. Some assume positions of leadership, directing the game from every angle. They call out who should be up at bat and who should be on deck as they envision plays and ultimately their team's victory unfold. Other kids simply follow the direction provided or stand on the sidelines cheering their classmates on. A few kids resent the power dynamics that have surfaced and argue about every call made throughout the game. Typically these tantrums end with a kid calling out "I quit" and finding peace in their tears under a shade tree with the comfort of extra attention now directed their way. The teachers and volunteers on recess duty have assumed the role of coaches. They try to keep peace, challenge the kids to play fair, and remind them often that "it's just a game."

"It's just a game."

When you are eight years old, it is not just a game. It is a matter of winning or losing, fitting in with your classmates, being accepted, and not making the mistake that costs your team the game. You let the words "it's just a game" pass through one ear and out the other for years. Then the day comes when you find yourself in a coaching role and those dreaded, disregarded words flow off your tongue. You grasp for your breath as though you have been sucker-punched in the gut and desperately try to recall the words. It's too late. Cynicism has set in and you realize in that moment that you have been brainwashed through the years.

"Game on," you say to yourself. You accept the challenge of proving that the pickup game of kickball, the crumbling relationship you are trying to save, and the cross-functional project at work are so much more than just a game. You acknowledge based on the wisdom that you have gained through the years that there does not need to be a winner and a loser in every situation. You remind yourself that competition has its place in life but we cannot become consumed by it. There are plenty of opportunities to find consensus with others, to achieve win-win results. The determining factor is whether you are willing to compromise and be open to others' ideas. Or if you find greater solace in shouting "I quit" and storming off to wallow in your self-pity. If you chose to wallow too often, I will warn you that the attention that you seek will wane and instead of solace, solitude will envelop you.

The fact is that you cannot win a game by yourself. Your own plays will only carry you so far. You will reach a point in the game where the ball will not be tossed your way. The coach will stop engaging your talent because the real power plays require more than your skills alone. Michael Jordan coaches, **"Talent wins games, but teamwork and intelligence wins championships."** The teams and coaches in your life want to win championships, and you have the power to decide if you make it to the championship team or not.

At their core, all of the team experiences that we have had mirror our recess memories. People naturally assume roles. Some direct while others motivate and cheer. Some coach while others sulk out of jealousy, insecurities, and fear. And some just play along while following the leader. Think about the role that you naturally assume when you enter collaboration. Do you take the lead in facilitating a discussion on the team's goals and objectives? Do you listen carefully and observe intently? Do you challenge assumptions and play devil's advocate? Each of us naturally assumes a role on a team based on our personalities, work ethic, and leadership style. **How we adjust our approach and engagement on a team is what ultimately influences and secures our place on a championship team.**

Many of us have probably attended a training program, perused a book or article, or listened to an expert on the topic of teamwork. I am sure that Bruce Tuckman's four stages of group development have surfaced at some point: "forming, storming, norming and performing." Maybe we have heard the cliché that "there is no I in team" or seen the popular image of geese flying in formation as a metaphor for teamwork. While all of these lessons can trigger reflection on effective teamwork, few drill down into the "how" of working collaboratively towards a common vision.

Many people advance through college, a post-secondary degree program and launch into their career without truly being taught how to work effectively with a team of people. All along the way, we are tasked with working in groups and we are judged on whether we were effective or not. Some make it on pure intuition, their talent and skills. Others who are naturally independent workers or processors struggle working in the moment, and they often find themselves running to catch up with the rest of the team. Through my experience, I have found that it is rare that someone takes the coaching reins and guides a diverse group of people through the process of building trust, establishing group norms, outlining and adopting a decision-making model, prioritizing tasks, delegating effectively, and holding each other accountable for the targeted deliverables.

Experience often becomes people's coach and the degree to which we are willing to engage in honest self-reflection determines how much we learn from each team initiative. Through my self-reflection, I call out the following ah-ha lessons for your consideration and application the next time you find yourself on a team.

1) **Do your homework.** Research and gather as much as you can about your teammates. Learn about their past experiences, networks, skills, work ethic, and personality. This data gives you a starting point to relate to each team member, common ground on which you can begin to build your foundation of trust and respect for each other. Dig into the team assignment as well by exploring similar projects that have unfolded. Sometimes the industry, field, or scope of work may not be a perfect match, but the process that was utilized could offer some valuable lessons learned. We have heard

the cliché, "Don't reinvent the wheel." Doing your homework sets you up for success by grounding you in past mistakes and effective practices.

2) **People matter**. People on your team do not equal the project or task at hand. Each of your teammates represents an individual that yearns to be heard, to be respected and to be valued. Start your teamwork by building trust with one another, acknowledging the lives and responsibilities that you each have outside of the team. The social interaction among teammates is critical to your team's success and should not unfold solely in the form of an ice breaker during your first team interaction. Rather, build in formal and informal activities and team habits that cultivate relationships in authentic ways over the course of your time together. Often times, these interactions serve as the catalyst for future collaboration.

3) **Be vulnerable**. Each of us has our own opinions and perspectives that are rooted in our experiences, values, and past lessons. When interacting with others, remember that they often do not have the same set of experiences, values and teachings. When they pose questions to us, they are seeking context and clarification. Assuming that they are judging us will only put us on the defensive. When we are vulnerable and open to exploring our perspectives out loud, we may discover that our opinions are not well grounded, we may reinforce our conviction to our beliefs, or we may gather context from others that further shapes our stance.

4) **Listen**. Hearing every team member's perspective ensures balance on a team. Otherwise the loudest and most outgoing team members rule the dialogue which transforms overtime into ruling the decisions and direction of the team. Effective teams often task someone with being the facilitator to ensure that everyone has the opportunity to share their ideas, concerns and recommendations. Patrick Lencioni, author of The Five Dysfunctions of a Team, writes, "It's as simple as this. When people don't unload their opinions and feel like they've been listened to, they won't really get on board."

5) **Focus**. Teams often get tripped up when the members of the team start moving in different directions and modify the desired end state or targeted deliverables in their minds. Keeping a strong focus

as a team on where the team needs to go and subsequently where each team member needs to contribute maintains a shared vision throughout the project. This requires that the team pauses and reflects often on priorities to ensure alignment. Maintaining focus does not mean that a team stifles new ideas along the way, but that it does so with an eye towards the team goals. One of the techniques that I have deployed often when working in teams is to develop a placemat outlining our vision, mission, goals and objectives. The tool can be referenced at each team meeting as reminder of what the team is aiming to accomplish. When new ideas surface, they can be filtered through the placemat to ensure alignment, and the placemat can function as a scorecard for individual team members reporting their progress on tasks that they are accountable for on the team.

There are certainly countless tips and tools to ensure the success of a team. The lessons that I shared above just skim the surface. However, I have consistently witnessed these practices missing from teams that I have been engaged with, and they are often what hold individual team members back from playing on the championship team.

"It's not just a game." It's a compilation of choices that we make while playing on a team that ultimately determines how others respect, engage and value us. It's how we consistently show up across multiple games that fosters our reputation, demonstrates our work ethic and lands us a role on the championship team.

So get on the team, keep your eye on the prize, and be a champion!

Take Action: Build Championship Teams

- Reflect on the various teams that you have been a part of and identify the role(s) that you have traditionally played or naturally gravitated towards. Were you the motivator that kept everyone engaged and excited about the project? Were you the leader that shaped the scope of the project and delegated tasks to your team members? Did you just follow along for the ride, completing whatever tasks were given to you? Consider how your role(s) have influenced the teams that you have been on and what you would have done differently if you were to rewind and play all over again.

- Consider the role of a leader and a follower. Identify the role that you most often play, and identify an opportunity to assume the other role in an upcoming project or through an outside activity. For example, if you naturally assume a leadership role, join a volunteer group that already has a leader and explore how you adjust (or don't adjust) to the role of a follower. Ask yourself what is easy and what is hard about assuming a different role. What do you learn about leadership through playing a different role?

Chapter 9: Manage People, Not Widgets

"Management is efficiency in climbing the ladder of success; leadership determines whether the ladder is leaning against the right wall."

-Stephen Covey

Across more than two decades, Oprah held the number one spot on television. She inspired us, cried with us, challenged us, laughed with us and demonstrated compassion each year as her fame and fortune grew. As her brand has grown to include a magazine, radio station and now an entire network, Oprah has transparently taken us on a journey through her struggles and celebrations while posing the hard questions that many of us grapple with in our own lives. She has called us to "live our best life" in our relationships, career, and spiritual journey. Oprah has reminded us that we are all human; we will make mistakes. She has pushed us to prioritize our response to obstacles versus dwelling on the obstacle itself.

When Oprah was asked to speak at Harvard's 2013 commencement ceremony, she provided some great insights on success and failure in the same style that we all have grown accustomed to from watching her through the years. For me, the thesis of her address was that all humans share a "common denominator in our human experience" regardless of race, gender, economic status or education level. We all seek to be validated.

"We want to be understood," taught Oprah. "I've done over 35,000 interviews in my career. And as soon as that camera shuts off, and inevitably in their own way, everyone asks this question: 'Was that okay?' I heard it from President Bush, I heard it from President Obama, I've heard it from heroes and from housewives. I've heard it from victims and perpetrators of crimes. I even heard it from Beyoncé in all her Beyoncé-ness … They all want to know: 'Was that okay? Did you hear me? Did you see me? Did what I say mean anything to you?'"

I have been drawn to Oprah's teaching about our human desire to be validated ever since I read her speech. I have seen this yearning for validation play out in corporate board rooms, inner-city classrooms, community-based collaborations, and in my own head. From the executive to the child living in poverty, we all want to know that what we do and say matters. We want to feel valued.

There are times when we escalate games over priorities and ego over impact. We play political games when we seek validation and are struggling to feel connected to people, to our work, and to our communities. By over-analyzing the words spoken to us, the tone of someone's voice, and the actions that unfold around us, our minds can spotlight an illusion that breeds insecurity. We question our abilities, our talent, and our purpose. We then overcompensate in our quest to matter that we put others down, highlighting their faults and passing blame. The irony of our actions is that in an effort to be validated we deprive someone else of the joy that blossoms when we feel heard, welcomed, and valued.

The Golden Rule calls us to treat others as we want to be treated. In our human experience, we must acknowledge that this behavior does not always flow naturally. We must check ourselves and invite others to call us out when our selfishness trumps compassion. To be validated, one must embrace their voice with confidence and share themselves with the world while acknowledging and seeking to learn from the stories that others share through their words and actions.

Listen more and seek to understand what is not being said. Look for opportunities to authentically and genuinely embrace the diversity of thought, feeling and experience that someone brings into your life. Be open to learning from others. Stand proudly and live out loud, elevating your voice and talents in a purpose-driven life. Validation stokes the fire in our bellies and gives light to our passion. It is our "common denominator."

As we advance in our careers from managing tasks to managing people, remembering our "common denominator" is even more relevant and necessary.

If you search the word "management" on Google, your search will result in 2.8+ billion results. Search for management books on Amazon and close to one million options are available. Look in the course catalogs of universities and you are bound to find a plethora of management classes designed to engage the newly appointed manager, the seasoned professional and everyone in between. Dozens of magazines focus their monthly editions on how to advance stronger management practices. The fact of the matter is that there is no shortage of information and training on how to succeed as a manager.

I have spent countless hours perusing articles, books, training programs, and coaching sessions in an attempt to foster and develop my management skills. In the end, the best source of training that I have found is hands-on learning, immersing myself into managing projects and teams in a variety of settings. Through my hands-on management experience, I have failed and I have succeeded. However, I still have dozens of questions and remain committed to learning and growing in developing my management skills.

In this chapter, I offer some key lessons that I have learned so far throughout my management journey. From managing a student council event to a corporate strategy to a nonprofit organization, these lessons represent parts of my management philosophy, and by deploying them, I am shaping my legacy. I encourage you to reflect on them, and challenge you to test drive them as you shape your own management philosophy.

#1: People are not widgets.

People matter...period. They have fears, aspirations, insecurities, and commitments outside of work. People want to be respected, engaged and valued. They want you to sincerely acknowledge their presence, contributions and commitment. Genuinely care about people. Challenge yourself to continually step into other people's shoes and look at the world through their perspective. Consider how your words (or lack thereof) will be translated in their minds. Treat people with compassion by employing empathy. Create a space where people can bring their whole self to the team. Remember and celebrate milestones like birthdays, employment anniversaries, weddings and births.

#2: Step away from your desk.

Roll up your sleeves and work alongside people. Experience what they experience. Challenge your assumptions. Gather context on what it takes for each person to meet performance goals by witnessing them in action. Andrew Carnegie once stated, "The older I get the less I listen to what people say and the more I look at what they do." Gather insight from people's actions on the front line.

#3: Question more and talk less.

Engage in the role of coach, advisor, or thought partner. Use questions to call out and challenge people's assumptions. Inquire about what is and is not working. Ask why. Clarify understanding and direction. Listen to what is not being said. Identify trends across team members. Clarify the big picture. When you are micro-managing, turn questions around and empower people to make decisions.

#4: Transparency builds trust.

Deliver the truth. Provide context. Admit what you don't know. Don't speculate or create rumors. Don't say something about someone else unless you have already told them directly. Stating you know something but cannot share it fosters power plays, breeds frustration and weakens collaboration.

#5: Get direct feedback.

Ask your team directly how you are managing. Embrace their feedback openly and often. Don't get defensive or make excuses. Just listen. Retain what is working. Reflect on what is not working and try a different approach. Pulse check your performance at the water cooler, over coffee or through desk-side chats.

#6: Remove obstacles.

Identify barriers to your team's performance. Brainstorm solutions together. Take the lead on removing hurdles. Verify that the obstacle has been removed. Differentiate between what is in your control versus what you can influence.

#7: Be authentic.

Commit to being the best "you." Humanize yourself by sharing and relating your personal and professional stories. Don't change your character depending on the scene and audience. Be consistent. Be present or don't show up.

#8: Push hard. Play hard.

Challenge people to achieve their potential. Stretch their performance. Put more faith in people than they have in themselves. Make good better and stretch better to become the best. Set challenging yet obtainable goals. Listen to advertising guru David Ogilvy's advice, "Look for people who will aim for the remarkable, who will not settle for the routine." Celebrate victory at each milestone. Laugh. Have fun together.

#9: Focus and prioritize.

Provide clarity on goals and direction on action. Drive efficiency and promote effective practices. Constantly prioritize to remain relevant and within a balanced workload. Set clear expectations. Maintain a scorecard. Put it all in writing as a desktop guide and reference it often.

#10: Feed people's hunger.

Consider John Quincy Adams' wisdom, "If your actions inspire others to dream more, learn more, do more and become more, you are a leader." Keep work fresh, engaging and challenging for your team. Acknowledge when greener pastures would elevate people and guide them there.

Overall, I believe that management is about getting grounded in why and focusing on how. Managers must understand the big picture (the why) to effectively guide their teams. They must also know how to operationalize a vision and strategy (the how) to efficiently get things done. When people on teams do not see the connection between their work and the bigger picture or purpose, they will often lose motivation and feel disconnected from the team and organization overall.

I have learned through my management experience that shaping clear expectations and being transparent with colleagues is a formula for success. Far too often, I have seen situations where team members are reprimanded for not performing at a certain level or producing a specific result when their manager did not clearly articulate expectations or the desired outcome. I always recommend seeking clarity on goals and expectations in writing so that you know what your scorecard looks like in the end.

Take Action: Manage People, Not Widgets

- Outside of perusing management articles and books as well as taking management classes, evaluate your own management experiences after the completion of major milestones. Consider what did and did not work for the team in terms of how you managed them and the project. Ask the team members for direct feedback as well (and remain open to hearing it when it is given). You could even reach out to previous employees you managed for their feedback. Keep a simple chart of "+" and "-" that you can refer to during each of your management opportunities. This exercise helps you practice self-reflection and avoid making mistakes over and over that negatively impact a team and a project.

- Consider all of the managers that you have had through the years and identify your own list of do's and don'ts based on those managers' actions. Strive to replicate the positive actions that contributed to a team and project's success.

Chapter 10: Empathize

"Being empathic means...that for the time being you lay aside the views and values you hold for yourself in order to enter another's world without prejudice...Perhaps this description makes clear that being empathic is a complex, demanding, strong yet subtle and gentle way of being."

-Carl Rogers

As the youngest of three boys, I can remember always wanting to follow in the footsteps of my older brothers. I wanted to race down the paths that they paved, tripping on their heels and experiencing the world with them. I did not want to live in their shadow or be put in my place. Rather, I aspired to be their equal, to be accepted by them and respected for what made me unique. My commitment to following their every move is what eventually directed me to discovering my passion for service. Through service I seeded an empathetic state of mind. Through acting, I nurtured that seed and the empathy within me grew strong roots that keeps me grounded today.

When my brothers were teenagers, they landed their first summer jobs working at a local YMCA camp for kids between the ages of 6 and 12. I hated the first summer when they both were employed, leaving the house early in the morning and not returning until late in the afternoon. When they came home, I wanted to play and they wanted to relax after entertaining kids all day. At dinner, they would recount stories of what happened at camp and what they were planning for the next day. I was so jealous of what they were doing without me, that I asked my older brother if I could volunteer at the camp. He pulled a few strings with the camp director, and I landed my first official volunteer role working with 6 year olds on a "trial" basis when I was 11. Tell me something is a "trial" and I give it everything I have to exceed expectations, which I did and found myself volunteering for several more years with my brothers.

Through my experience volunteering at the YMCA, I not only got to work with the 6 year olds, but I also had the opportunity to work one on one with a young boy with Down's syndrome. Each day, I felt a sense of purpose. All of "my" kids were relying on me to plan and assist with various games and activities. Whether they had fun or felt like they were in summer school depended partly on me, and I accepted that challenge very seriously. Being so close in age, I put myself in their shoes and tasked myself with generating ideas that would relate to their interests and fully engage them.

Over several summers in my volunteer role, I honed in on my creativity and learned an important life lesson. Each kid that I worked with had a story, and the words and behaviors that appeared on the surface only told half of their story. Beneath the surface laid emotions and experiences that, if I could tap into those, I discovered that I could establish trust, sustain respect, and more fully engage the whole child in our programs. In essence, I discovered empathy.

Through additional volunteer experiences working with senior citizens at a local nursing home, I fueled my passion for service and explored empathy further. I recall one woman specifically that holds a special place in my heart. Her name was Kathy, and she was suffering from Alzheimer's disease. Each Tuesday that I would arrive to assist with Bingo, arts and crafts or game days, Kathy would be sitting at the front door waiting for me. Each Tuesday, I played a different role in Kathy's mind. Sometimes I was her husband and we were just dating. On other days, I was Kathy's son who she was scolding for missing his curfew. Occasionally, I played my own role as a teenager who had come to spend time with Kathy, reminding her how special she was and that I cared about her. Regardless of the roles that I played, I learned to not judge Kathy or be afraid of what she would say. Rather, I embraced Kathy with a warm smile, accepted her for who she was, and did not define her by the disease that was affecting her memory, thinking and behavior. I simply sought to understand her and to show compassion.

When I was in high school, I joined the Forensics (speech and debate) league and discovered a passion for acting, for embracing the roles of characters whose lives related to mine. It was through acting that I further explored empathy as I challenged myself to crawl into the skin, mind and soul of each character I portrayed. I wanted desperately to view the world through the characters' eyes, to feel what they felt and to move as they would move.

Acting inspired me to explore empathy through my own writing. In short stories and poetry, I transform myself into other characters and challenge myself to convey their thoughts, feelings, and desires. I read all that I can on the subjects of my writing, embrace the stories of characters similar to mine, and then breathe life onto a page with my words.

While visiting San Francisco on a business trip, I went jogging downtown one morning and was struck by the number of homeless veterans living on the streets. Back in my hotel room, I drew from the empathy that I was feeling and wrote the following poem.

A Freedom Anthem

From the Garden of Eden to the streets of San Francisco,
we meet again.
Raised with a freedom dream,
called to duty in pursuit of justice,
We sacrificed.
We suspended our values.
We killed.
We survived.

Scars torture our minds
with recollections of blood, sweat and tears
Reenactments of the battlefield loop continuously...
surface spontaneously
The slightest reminders...the taste...the smell...the sounds.

We live on the edge,
teetering between the past and the present.
Our future is dependent on our own strength
and other's compassion.

I play a tune, a freedom anthem.
Plucking the strings like I plucked landmines
from the war zone
carefully...methodically...in a focused rhythm
I sweep the streets with my music.

Into their eyes I stare...
recognizing their innocence, their guilt.
Recalling my sins and begging forgiveness,
my melodies play on
The majority walk on,
discarding the truth like trash on the street.

My fingers work the keys like they worked the trigger
quickly
without breathing
then a sigh of relief
for dodging the bullet
for keeping the beat
I survived.

My brothers and sisters throw money and food
like soldiers throw bombs.
These band aids for peace don't stop the bleeding.
They cover the pain.
They prolong the misery.
The quest for freedom
is nothing more than a dream
and now I stand forgotten.

Don't toss me your pity or your petty change.
Lend me your hand.
Lift my spirits with your genuine concern.
With the recognition that as long as I lie quietly on the street
or bantering in the allies of your high rises
covered with boxes from your privileged purchases
nibbling on scraps found in your garbage
I am trying to survive on a thread of dignity
On the honor that I pledged to uphold
As a soldier sent off to fight for your freedom.

Let my music stand as a reminder
that the beauty in my soul,
the talent in my fingers,
the opportunity in my mind,

Need acknowledged and nurtured.

I live
I breath
I dream

I am a volunteer and a veteran of a war,
returned from a battlefield that is far less cold,
less inhumane than the streets where I now reside.

I play music,
a melody that flows like a white flag to surrender.
I am grasping at a childhood dream of freedom
and wondering if you replaced me on these streets,
what music would you play,
what note would you hold onto?

Through a great deal of self-reflection, I have discovered that **empathy, when nurtured and practiced, shapes our values, influences our motivation, and energizes our passion.** Just as each of us desires to be heard, to be understood, others desire the same regardless of the hardships that they have stumbled on or the tough exteriors that they hide behind. At home, at work, in school, or in our community, we want to feel connected to people who genuinely care about us. When we feel respected, we respect others and value their contributions and their unique voice and talents. **When empathy is deployed in abundance, there is a transparency that unfolds that serves as a thread that weaves our society together across cultures.**

The empathy we practice strengthens our ability to influence and spark change. Stephen Covey writes, "The real beginning of influence comes as others sense you are being influenced by them – when they feel understood by you – that you have listened deeply and sincerely, and that you are open." Life is a series of give and take exercises. **Empathy is a muscle that, when strengthened, sustains balances in our point of view. Otherwise we are misguided by the singularity of our**

own perspective which lacks education from the minds and experiences of others.

When we practice empathy, it is important to note that we are not necessarily agreeing with someone else or stating to them that we understand what they are going through. Rather, we are suspending our judgment to genuinely explore their point of view and seeking to understand the roots of their perspective. This action fosters more grounded discussions and compassionate engagements.

Albert Einstein's perspective on empathy highlights the interconnectedness of humans and calls us to action by exploring the world beyond our own limited experiences. He writes, "A human being is a part of a whole, called by us 'universe,' a part limited in time and space. He experiences himself, his thoughts and feelings as something separated from the rest... a kind of optical delusion of his consciousness. This delusion is a kind of prison for us, restricting us to our personal desires and to affection for a few persons nearest to us. Our task must be to free ourselves from this prison by widening our circle of compassion to embrace all living creatures and the whole of nature in its beauty."

I remain committed to continually widening my "circle of compassion" by practicing empathy in my daily life. I am certainly not perfect and find myself rushing to judgment at times. In those moments, I try to pause and diversify my view by getting grounded in the views and experiences of others. I look for examples of people who practice empathy and seek inspiration from their words and actions.

Recently I witnessed a beautiful act of kindness. There was a young woman speaking to a homeless man on the corner who was asking each passerby for spare change or food. She paused to speak to the man and asked, "What would you like to eat?" After taking his order, she went to Starbucks and returned a few moments later to hand the man a large coffee equipped with cream and sugar along with a blueberry muffin. She wished the man well and walked off down the sidewalk.

It certainly is admirable that the young woman paused to help the homeless man, and it was even more inspiring that she paused to take his order. She treated him with dignity, and she acknowledged that few have asked this man how they could help him. Some toss change in his cup while others smile politely as they pick up their pace strolling by. Most ignore the man and disregard the stories that comprise the chapters in his life. They predict a future of begging, disease, and unfortunate circumstances rather than ignite hope in this man's spirit.

I pray each day for peace – peace of mind, peace in our schools and communities, peace among nations competing for power – so that the human race can co-exist and that the compassion we show one another ignites hope and inspiration that is passed from generation to generation. While we wait patiently for others to embrace the kindness that we seek, let us choose to ask those around us, "how may I help you?" If we can each pause to acknowledge our interconnectedness with one another, then through our acts of compassion, we will serve as a beacon of hope and spark a fire of change that spreads from heart to heart and mind to mind.

Take Action: Empathize

- Immerse yourself in a new culture or community. Explore the people's traditions, food, dress, habits, etc. Suspend all judgment and focus on trying to fully "walk a mile in someone else's shoes." Respectfully ask questions to dig below the surface in your immersion.

- Read a diverse array of biographies to better understand people, their motivations, their fears, and their dreams. Seek to clarify why they made the decisions that they did and how the consequences of their decisions shaped their lives and the lives of others.

- Suspend your judgment of others and practice asking more questions to better understand the context behind people's perspectives and decisions. For example, think of someone or a group that you have felt intimidated by or have been unable to empathize with and reach out to them with questions that demonstrate your desire to learn. Ask about how they formed their opinions or what has influenced their values. Inquire about what has reinforced their opinions and values as well as examples of times when they themselves questioned their beliefs.

Chapter 11: Go to the Front Line

"If your actions inspire others to dream more, learn more, do more and become more, you are a leader."

-John Quincy Adams

I have always had a great deal of respect for reporters that venture to the front lines of a news story. Some risk their own lives during times of turmoil and war to give voice to conflict by showcasing the emotions and perspectives of those engaged and affected. When disasters strike around the world, photographers and videographers capture a million words in their photos and footage spurring action to the front lines amongst a world of volunteers and donors. Similarly, the writers and producers of documentaries explore issues from the front line or profile individuals by interviewing those closest to them in order to share diverse points of view and challenge our assumptions. Detectives investigate their cases from the front line to piece together the truth and advance justice. Case managers work tirelessly on the front line to equip individuals with tools to succeed and to remove obstacles from their paths. Parents go to the front lines of their kids' lives by using their intuition to determine the root causes of sour moods and bad behavior.

Over the course of my career, I have found tremendous value in venturing to the front line. As a nonprofit executive, I have asked front line program staff to join me at board meetings and donor discussions. When I transitioned to corporate philanthropy, I often asked to meet with senior leadership from a nonprofit along with a staff person working on the front line of the organization's programs. Senior leadership provides insight on mission, context on the problem(s) being addressed, and high level strategies. Front line staff share stories of real people engaged in programs. They provide insight into what is working and what is missing from the strategies being employed. The staff can identify the trends across the client base which should align with how an organization is shaping their strategies and programs. Smart organizations realize that this balanced perspective provides greater clarity on their work, results and needs in order to fulfill their mission. In my case, this perspective creates a more compelling case to engage, support and invest. The front line knowledge and experience equips me with the context to communicate more clearly about an issue, an organization or a person whose story I want to share with others.

When leadership prioritizes spending time on the front line, they gain insight into what is working and what is holding their organizations back. They foster partnerships with talent that can be more fully utilized in solving problems, developing new products or approaches, and growing to scale and potential. They gain respect among their team for not isolating themselves in an ivory tower but rather grounding themselves in the trenches of reality.

Leaders that acknowledge their own limitations and seek clarity on issues and perspectives from their team gain my respect. Through 30 minute phone calls with team members across the organization's hierarchy, leaders can keep their eye on team morale. By engaging in volunteer projects with cross-functional teams, leaders can cultivate relationships and foster greater loyalty with talent. In town hall sessions, leaders can celebrate results and team member contributions that shape organizational culture. Over coffee, breakfast, lunch or dinner, leaders can test their assumptions, rally support for new ideas, hear firsthand how team members are spending their time, and identify emerging talent. Leaders that regularly engage with the front line of their organizations acknowledge that people matter. When people feel as though they matter, they are more committed to adding value and strive to deliver their full potential.

Watch some episodes of "Undercover Boss" and you will start to see the value of what I am sharing here. The CEOs in some cases were surprised by what they discovered on the front line, and the experience served as a wake-up call to deepen their engagement at all levels of their business. They strengthened their employee training programs, enhanced customer service platforms, and fixed inefficiencies in their processes. In other cases, they discovered rock star employees, untapped talent that could fast track their growth if given the opportunity to lead. They went through the customer experience and saw firsthand how customers were engaged and treated. Venturing outside of their executive suites proved to be time well spent, and the experience sparked a new found appreciation for the front line.

In a country where our education system is struggling to reinvent itself from the industrial age, I find hope in superintendents and principals that prioritize spending time in the classroom with teachers and students. They witness firsthand effective teaching practices, innovative uses of technology and creative classroom management techniques. These school leaders gather examples of great teachers to spotlight at professional development workshops, school board meetings and PTO sessions. Beyond the student performance quantitative data, they not only gather qualitative reviews from the students directly about how they are learning but also ideas for improving school culture and student engagement.

Regardless of the industry, the front line is a learning laboratory that is too often left underexplored and underutilized. Front line team members are untapped talent and may be dismissed by leaders that have lost sight of key success measures and are blinded by their inflated egos. These leaders assume that they have all of the answers and may ultimately disrespect the team members whose talent helps promote their success.

When I first started my consulting and speaking business, I recognized right away from my own experience that front line team members are underinvested in across multiple sectors and fields. There are countless programs, seminars and classes for senior leadership, but there are few programs designed specifically for front line talent. Further, I noticed a trend in the private sector where "owning your own professional development" was a value often promoted during new hire orientation and annual performance management cycles. I understand the importance of being personally motivated to learn and grow, but I have also witnessed many front line team members that simply are not aware of what they need to grow, to discover and to reach their full potential. Perhaps a little more investment in the coaching of front line talent would accelerate their development, maximize their contributions and deliver unprecedented results.

William Shakespeare's famous monologue from *As You Like It* reminds us that "All the world's a stage, and all the men and women merely players, they have their exits and entrances; and one man in his time plays many parts." We all have a part to play in life, at home with family, in our circle of friends, at work, and in our communities. At times, some parts will be bigger than others. We will have more lines and stand longer in the spotlight. There will be times when our lines are cut. We will be directed to stand in the shadows as part of the chorus or we may find ourselves offstage supporting the play behind the scenes. We must not forget that each part is important and contributes to the overall success of the play on life. **By challenging ourselves to explore each role and acknowledge each role's unique contributions to the whole, we will attain rave reviews.**

Step outside of your current role and mindset. Venture to the front line. Look around and observe what is happening. Ask questions, listen, and seek to understand. Humbly ask for advice, feedback, and ideas. Learn and grow. Embrace and engage. Deliver maximum results based on the insight and relationships that you foster on the front line.

Take Action: Go to the Front Line

- When researching an issue, go to individuals on the front line and ask great questions. Regardless of whether the issue pertains to parenting, being a student or working in a for profit or nonprofit organization, asking those with front line experience for clarity on their perspective, their experiences, will often deliver great insight for you in shaping your own perspective. As a youth advocate, I am always shocked when I visit youth-serving organizations that do not engage youth in their decision making process and program development work. Businesses that excel at customer service often engage their customers in shaping their brand and products.

- Watch documentaries. Documentaries are often a great source of front line perspective covering a wide variety of topics. Use documentaries to expand the information that you gather when forming your own perspective on issues.

- Volunteer for organizations that are addressing issues that you care about. By engaging in your community more frequently, you often expand your network and learn more about the issues at play that are propelling your neighborhood forward or negatively impacting it. As opposed to being an observer, you roll up your sleeves and become an active participant on the front line.

Chapter 12: Influence Change

*"There is nothing more difficult to take in hand,
more perilous to conduct, or more uncertain in its success, than to take
the lead in the introduction
of a new order of things."*

-Niccolo Machiavelli

Change is inevitable and can either be embraced or fought with all our might and mind. Sometimes, when we fight change too hard, we drive ourselves further away from the end point that we desired in the very beginning. We lose sight of what is important and become consumed and comfortable in tradition rather than challenging ourselves to strike out on new paths, explore new concepts and strategies and grow with the world around us.

Machiavelli stated, "Whoever desires constant success must change his conduct with the times."

Throughout my career in both nonprofit management and corporate community relations, I have been on a tireless pursuit to understand how to best address complex social issues. In mobilizing volunteers and investing financial resources, I have certainly managed to lend people and communities a hand in the short term. After years of studying issues and facilitating action both individually and collaboratively, I find myself deeply reflecting on how I can influence change at the root cause of issues and for longer term sustainability.

To influence change, I believe that volunteers, donors, organizers and community leaders need to focus on five key drivers: data, milestones, multi-layered investments, root causes, and innovation.

Data: Decisions that we make on where we invest, how we spend our volunteer time, what programs we close, launch or continue, and which organizations and issues that we advocate for should be based on solid, trustworthy data. While far too many organizations see program and organizational evaluations as a "nice to have" but not necessary, I see it as the baseline that separates organizations and individuals that are serious about influencing change and those that may mean well but have perhaps a different set of priorities.

In order to advance preventative tactics and reactive interventions for homeless individuals or families, we need to understand the data around the issue: what are the primary causes of homelessness, what supports have proven most effective, what practices in shelters lead to desired results, and what factors prevent chronic homelessness. Further, in education, we must start where the students, teachers, parents, and school leadership are in order to advance the necessary reforms. This requires that we start with some baseline data to understand how the students are currently performing, what support teachers are and are not getting, what resources the principal has at his or her hands, and what dilemmas are the parents facing which effect the home life of the student.

Data drives more informed decisions, and more informed decisions drive more comprehensive solutions.

Milestones: I believe that it is human nature to want short term victories. In pursuit of the top grade in a class, we study hard for each test. In pursuit of a dream career, we strive to succeed in each position up the ladder. Similarly in tackling complex social issues, I believe that we need to focus on and celebrate milestones.

In education reform, I read a lot about "cradle to career" and calling attention to the milestones in between that are predictors of success. For example, if a child enters school with the ability to read, they have achieved an early education milestone and are more likely to successfully graduate on time. In workforce development, individuals that earn credentials such as certifications are more marketable and typically earn higher wages. These credentials are milestones in an individual's career.

By focusing on milestones, I believe that we take complex issues and solutions and make them manageable to address. If we work collaboratively with others, we can assist individuals in tackling milestones at a faster and more efficient rate...ultimately ensuring that they stay on their path to success.

Multi-layered Investments: I believe that we as a society far too often toss money at problems in hopes that they will either be solved or somehow disappear. The reality is that money alone cannot solve social issues. I believe strongly that money is essential in combination with human resources that provide time and talent. Mobilizing leaders to serve on boards, engaging talented experts on well-defined projects, and galvanizing volunteers to assist in implementing or supporting programs all deepen investments of money and maximize our impact.

Layering investments takes time, trust, and strategic thinking that may feel as though a solution is getting too complicated. However, I believe solutions to complex issues should not feel easy and deeper relationships ensure longer lasting partnerships and often high quality solutions.

Root Causes: While our resources and time may be limited, I believe it is critical to influence change for good by focusing on both short term solutions and root causes which make issues so complex. In a poor economic community that is isolated from the center of an urban community, advancing workforce skills is not enough. People need access to affordable and reliable transportation along with jobs that align with their current skills and abilities. Getting a computer program certificate is not fully helping someone if they can't get to a job three towns away since there are no IT jobs in their own community. And if they are illiterate, obtaining the computer certificate is incredibly difficult. If we invest our money in short term solutions, we should consider how we can invest our time in root causes by increasing awareness around the complexity of the issue and mobilizing others to influence change in root causes.

Innovation: It is critical to advance data-based decisions and support research-backed programs and solutions. I equally believe it is important to invest in innovation. Proven practices work for some but may not work for all. Further, they may not advance the most cost-effective solution and take advantage of the full breadth of partnerships and resources that can be leveraged in any situation. Therefore, by focusing on innovation, we are constantly challenging our assumptions, testing the scalability of solutions, and adjusting to the changing times and nuances of the complex issues we are tackling. Innovation also spurs attention of individuals who may join us in our pursuit to influence change.

Data, milestones, multi-layered investments, root causes and innovation all elevate our ability to influence the change we wish to see. As someone that focuses on complex issues every day and sometimes feels overwhelmed in pursuit of sustainable change, I think that these five drivers can push us as a society to remain focused on solid solutions and not band aid interventions. These drivers inform an investment strategy that I believe would certainly differentiate one from many other donors, volunteers, organizers and community leaders. Perhaps our attention and integration of these drivers into our own plans and actions can spur a movement among others so that we may all maximize our influencing change practices.

Take Action: Influence Change

- Explore the lives of those who have influenced change by reading their biographies and autobiographies. Immerse yourself in their stories and evaluate the trends that emerge in how they make decisions and interact with others.

- Create a collage using portraits of those that you identify as influencers. They can be famous individuals, political leaders, business entrepreneurs, family members and friends. Position the collage at home or at work as a visual reminder of their impact and the influence that you can advance.

Chapter 13: Jog and Sprint

*"A journey of a thousand miles
must begin with a single step."*

-Lao Tzu

While many of us try hard to make life a continual sprint, life has taught me that the journey we are on should unfold more like a marathon. The older I get, the more I savor each step of the journey and value all that goes into successfully completing one. I am challenging myself to balance my jogging and sprinting so that I don't bypass opportunities, relationships and experiences that contribute to leading a life of purpose.

The journey of those that run marathons begins with an important step, the decision to commit to the journey. The attitude that fuels this decision sustains the individual to and across the finish line.

There is a great deal of training and practice that unfolds over months leading up to the race. During this time, runners call upon the advice and support of coaches and supporters to strengthen their bodies and minds as they push onwards. Marathoners reach moments where their internal voice elevates excuses for why they shouldn't or can't complete the journey. Their perseverance triumphs over this persuasion and they race onward.

The runners wear their numbers with pride, which represent their unique lot, their individuality, in this world. They approach the starting line both as an individual and a team full of determination to succeed and anxiety over the unknown.

Water stations and motivators line the course breathing life into their tired lungs. Unexpected hurdles creep up along the course, yet their confidence heals their injuries and satisfies their thirst. Marathoners embrace their mental dialogue, teetering between words of discouragement and words of endurance.

They hit the one mile marker to the finish line and joy envelops their weak body, propelling them forward to complete the journey with a sense of accomplishment and a rush of self-confidence. They cross the finish line to a thunderous applause from the crowd and a sense of personal satisfaction in completing their journey which began months earlier with the first step.

Each journey we take in life begins with the commitment we make to take the first step, to embrace the attitude of a winner who believes in their potential. Let us all recall the wise affirmation of Saturday Night Live character Stuart Smalley, "I'm good enough, I'm smart enough, and dog-gone it, people like me." **Then let's get to training our minds and bodies for the marathon of life, balancing jogging and sprinting to sustain our energy, seize opportunities, and savor relationships.**

Jog on, my friend! And then sprint!

Take Action: Jog and Sprint

- Watch Derek Sivers' TED Talk titled, "How to start a movement." As the video unfolds, Derek highlights how one individual quickly gains the attention and engagement of others showcasing the power and influence of both leaders and followers. I view the video as a reminder that if I sprint through life, I miss out on all of the "movements" around me where I could gain both inspiration and direction.

- Revisit your list of "someday I will do that" activities and make a commitment to do one of those activities today. Perhaps you have a friend that you haven't called in a long time. Pick up the phone and give him/her a call. Maybe you keep postponing the start of a diet. Get rid of the junk food in your pantry today and replace it with some fresh fruit and vegetables from a local farmer's market. Whatever the activities are, pick one and do it today rather than waiting for "someday" in the future.

- Set milestones for your long term goals. Figure out what goals you want to accomplish in the next 5-10 years. Now break those goals out into smaller, shorter term milestones that will move you towards the bigger, longer term goal. Keep breaking your goals down into smaller and smaller steps until you feel motivated to take the first step. Make it something realistic that you could accomplish in a week or a month. Take the necessary step and celebrate your accomplishment of short term milestones. Keep jogging to victory!

Chapter 14: Charge Through with Optimism

"When I was a boy and I would see scary things in the news, my mother would say to me, "Look for the helpers. You will always find people who are helping." To this day, especially in times of "disaster," I remember my mother's words and I am always comforted by realizing that there are still so many helpers – so many caring people in this world."

-Fred Rogers

Pessimism has made an unwavering commitment to weave its way into our lives and our minds. It broadcasts live through our newscasts that feature journalists racing to scenes of disasters in hopes of reporting first, capturing the exclusive interview or rolling the "never been seen" video clips and images. Our newspapers and magazines present feature articles and emotionally charged photographs that slowly chip away at our optimism with each conclusion that things will keep getting worse. The gossip shared in hair salons, grocery store lines and coffee shops serves as a continual reminder that love does not last, political promises will forever be broken and community trust is unlikely when we do not even know our neighbors' names.

With each tragic shooting, violent protest and painful speech, we can find ourselves becoming immune to the seriousness of each story until we are jolted by an even greater, more sensationalized tragedy that unfolds. In spotlighting those that seek fame and recognition, we place into the shadows those that serve our world as selfless helpers. These helpers move quickly to lend a hand, embrace a victim and care for the fallen. They seek no recognition and are armed with compassion. Their optimism is strong, and the prize they seek is an understanding that all humans are interconnected and interdependent on one another. These helpers build community and inspire people in the moments where pessimism believes it has triumphed.

For many of us, the greatest pessimist in our lives is not a journalist, a colleague at work or a family member. **Our internal voice can be our greatest deterrent from the optimism that can fuel our passion in life, drive the change we aspire to influence, and equip us with the courage to take risks.** We often give in to our internal voice which tends to feed on the pessimism in the world around us. We become victim to it, believing we do not have the skills and strength to achieve our dreams.

Much like great athletes that train for their championship games or musicians that practice countless hours for their award winning performances, **we must train our minds to block pessimism and**

instead embrace optimism. This is no easy task and is only accomplished with great discipline and consistently strengthening the habit.

One strategy for embracing a more optimistic attitude is to keep a gratitude journal in which we track and reflect on the positive things that we have encountered each day. Did someone compliment your work, attire or attitude? Did someone buy you lunch or offer you a homemade treat? Was someone kind on the road or perhaps hold a door for you? Did a colleague recognize you for your contributions on a project at work? There are positive things that happen to each of us, and it becomes easier to reflect on them when we are intentionally seeking them out to add to our gratitude journal.

While gratitude journaling helps us to reflect on those positive things that happen to us, advancing random acts of kindness for others proactively engages us in fostering a more optimistic culture. Random acts of kindness can be as simple as buying someone a cup of coffee or paying for another car's tolls on the highway. You can bake cookies for your colleagues at work or compliment someone who is delivering exceptional customer service. These acts of kindness empower your own attitude to be more optimistic as you seek to spread compassion versus complaints. Your acts can distract someone from dwelling on pessimistic thoughts and remind them that there are "helpers" all around striving to create a more optimistic society.

We can pay attention to the words that we use which carry great power in effecting both our own attitudes as well as the attitudes of others. For example, I have trained myself to replace the word "problem" with "opportunity." As cliché as that may be, I have noticed a difference in how I approach obstacles that arise in my life. If I address the obstacle by mentally considering it as an opportunity, I find my mind focusing on solutions and innovation. When we view obstacles as problems, we often focus on who is to blame for creating the problem and all the reasons why it will be difficult to overcome.

When considering the role of language in advancing optimism, I also reflect on the life advice that many of us have received stating, "If you don't have something nice to say, don't say anything at all." This is a reminder of how influential our words can be in shaping our own attitudes and the actions of others. Just pause and think about the last time that someone said something negative to you. You most likely were put on the defense, were hurt by the words spoken, and thought about the conversations long after it had ended. There is an example of how easy it is for pessimism to weasel its way into our minds and breed thoughts of self-doubt. **We condition ourselves to focus on our weaknesses rather than embracing our strengths and advancing our unique gifts with those around us.**

Marcus Buckingham has been leading a movement in the business world on a strengths-based approach. He calls for his audiences to focus their attention on those activities that engage their individual strengths versus consuming the majority of our time trying to fix our areas of weakness. As a community organizer at heart, I have made the connection between Marcus's work and what I believe to be a key strategy in developing and sustaining communities. When you focus on a community's strengths and assets, you start from a state of empowerment. Residents do not dwell on their needs but focus instead on what they can offer their community in shaping and advancing a more engaged society. **When each of us feels valued and as though we are contributing to something greater than ourselves in a meaningful way, a powerful transformation can occur.**

Winston Churchill once said, "A pessimist sees the difficulty in every opportunity; an optimist sees the opportunity in every difficulty." Despite the vast presence of pessimism in the world around us, we can foster a more optimistic society. By intentionally seeking out examples of optimistic behavior, we shift our minds and attitudes and discover an immense amount of opportunity around us. Focusing on our strengths versus our weaknesses gives us the courage to charge forward towards our dreams. Advancing acts of kindness inspires a change from within that sparks a movement of optimism among those impacted by our example. **Optimism gives us permission to charge through the obstacles that pessimism places before us, and it fuels our decision to live out our full potential.**

Take Action: Charge Through with Optimism

- Create a gratitude journal where you record daily those things and people for whom you are grateful. Reflect back throughout your day and recall those moments where you gained energy, support, direction, and/or a sense of satisfaction. After a few days, you will find yourself focused more on the positive aspects of your life versus the negative, energy-draining situations. You will begin to identify those individuals that fuel your energy versus those that drain your energy. Spend more time with those that lift you up for your optimism to soar.

- Practice random acts of kindness. Seek out opportunities to brighten someone else's day, to show someone that they are cared for, and to challenge them to pay it forward. Random acts of kindness can be as simple as holding a door or elevator for someone. You can surprise a co-worker, roommate, or partner with a cup of coffee. You can drop an unexpected, hand-written "thinking of you" note in the mail. Regardless of what you do, practicing random acts of kindness can spread optimism and enhance our own attitudes.

- Pick up a copy of Tom Rath's StrengthsFinder2.0 or make a list of your personal strengths. Paying attention to our body language can be a great indicator of when we are engaging our strengths. We tend to sit up straight, lean in, and sit on the edge of our seats. We can lose track of time when engaging our strengths and feel energized. Maximize the time in which you play to your strengths.

Chapter 15: Don't Burn Out

"Life is all memory, except for the one present moment that goes by you so quickly you hardly catch it going."

-Tennessee Williams

Hit the pause button on your life. Sit down in a quiet room. Turn off your phone. Close your laptop or turn off your iPad. Take off your headphones, and shut off the television. Sit in silence for a few moments and try to let your mind unwind and relax.

Did your eyes dart around the room from object to object? Did the items on your to do list pop into mind, slowly raising your blood pressure with each looming deadline recalled? Did you start to fidget or reposition yourself out of the discomfort of sitting still? Did new ideas come flooding into your mind? Were you uncomfortable sitting in silence?

I recently got in my car after a full day of back-to-back meetings and caught myself immediately trying to figure out what I was going to listen to on the ride home. I first tuned into NPR, changed the channel to CNN, moved on to top 20 hits, and then I loaded a CD from SUCCESS Magazine (yes, I said CD...remember those?). And then it dawned on me that what I really needed was silence. So I turned off the radio, shut off my phones (yes, plural...as if one phone is not enough), and began driving without a sound. It was in that moment that I realized how seldom I sit in silence, and how programmed we are as a society to fill every waking moment with noise.

Our daily routine may consist of running between meetings, calls or classes. We may find ourselves frantically trying to get out the door to run errands, pick up the kids, walk the dog, run to the grocery store or beat traffic. We answer emails while sitting on conference calls (don't deny it, we all do it). We scarf down meals while reading reports or prepping for our next meeting, dodging questions flying at us from colleagues in the office, on email or on IM. At lunch with a colleague or friend, we find ourselves texting or sending tweets to someone else.

Amidst all of this action and noise, we often find ourselves craving some quiet time, an opportunity to sit in silence by ourselves and let our minds catch up to where we are. We crave time to just sit and think. We are so busy running from one request or task to another that we barely have time to use the restroom let alone pause and gather our thoughts.

How have we allowed ourselves to be so programmed, so connected by technology yet so disconnected from our own minds? I feel like the pendulum has shifted; **in our quest to connect with each other and with people around the world, we have lost our connection with ourselves**. There is a striking lack of balance in many of our lives as we struggle to deliver perfection and juggle all of the commitments we have up in the air. In the end, we often reach a state of burnout.

I can speak from firsthand experience. I am a victim of self-induced burnout, having committed myself to delivering perfection in each project I tackle for years now. Rewinding all the way back to high school, I can remember getting an A on a test and feeling disappointed that I did not get the A+. If I came in second place, I beat myself up at practice to get first place in the next competition. When I wrote a paper, I would review and revise it ten times over before I felt it was acceptable to submit (and I still wouldn't be fully happy with it).

My quest for perfection intensified as I got older. Having launched a nonprofit at the age of 18, I felt like there was no room for error or else I would be labeled a failure or "unqualified" to lead the organization. Working in inner-city neighborhoods, I also felt the pressure to meet the needs of the kids we were engaging in our programs despite how complicated their lives were in their homes.

The pressure that I put on myself translated to my team, and that was not fair to them. Nothing was ever good enough, and I never paused to reflect on or celebrate the change that we were advancing. Rather, I kept pushing for more and consequently lost some great talent as I was learning how to lead both myself and others.

I learned the hard way that when you continue to fall more and more out of balance, you start to recognize the effects of stress on how you feel physically and mentally. At times you feel sick, weak, and drained. Your relationships suffer in that you spend less time with friends and family. When you are together, your mind is somewhere else, you are glued to your phone, or you lack patience with people because of your own exhaustion. Your exercise commitment drops, poor eating habits are developed as you eat on the run, and your health suffers. Despite hearing the same advice over and over again from coaches, mentors and managers to find balance and set more realistic goals, I, like many others, ignored the warnings and the advice.

The truth is that the more you try to deliver on unrealistic expectations or goals across the various dimensions of your life, the more likely the quality of your investments in each dimension will go down. Think about your 24 hours a day in a pie chart. If you continually invest more and more time at work, you are left with less time to divide across other dimensions like your social life, your faith, and your own health and wellness. Not only is your time diminished, but the quality of your time is also depleted. When you put in longer hours and feel more pressure at work, you have less energy and will be less present in the time you spend across the other dimensions.

Plato stated, "The part can never be well unless the whole is well." **We have to acknowledge that we cannot switch on and off each part of our wellbeing; these parts are interconnected.** Think about the child who comes to school in the morning wearing what he wore yesterday, having slept on the floor, and not having access to a nourishing dinner at night. How will that child most likely behave at school? Consider a business executive who is in the middle of a nasty divorce and fighting a custody battle over his two children. How will these personal affairs affect the executive's ability to focus at work, to provide direction, and to foster collaboration among departments?

I often say that people are like giant icebergs found out in the ocean. While you see them at the surface, what lies beneath is so much deeper and more complex. **When we invite others to bring their whole self to class, to work, to our relationships, we give people permission to make balanced decisions in their lives.** We take away the pressure to invest 100% in work or school and acknowledge that investments need to be made in our social, spiritual and physical dimensions as well. We show our respect for the choices that people make and provide them encouragement along their quest to obtain balance.

Achieving balance is not easy, and it is a lifelong quest. I believe that it is easy though to pause and reflect on the investments that you are making across the various dimensions of your life. Acknowledge where you are over or under investing and make the choices necessary to avoid burnout.

I challenge you, just like I challenge myself, to embrace silence, to create more opportunities to pause and enjoy it, and to not enter into silence with the expectation that you will be productive in generating new ideas, additional projects, or further action. Rather, your time in silence will give you a chance to breath, relax and remind yourself that a little **me time** every once in a while serves the mind, body and soul in ways that few other tasks on the to-do list can deliver.

Take Action: Don't Burn Out

- Take time for silent reflection every day. Even if you can only carve out 10 minutes of silence, do it. Unplug from all of your devices and be present somewhere with few distractions. Allow your mind to savor the silence. Pay attention to your breathing and just sit still. These silent reflections will slow you down long enough to discover a peaceful state of mind and challenge you to live more in the present.

- The University of California Riverside defines "seven dimensions of wellness" that they believe contribute to our quality of life: social, emotional, spiritual, environmental, occupational, intellectual, and physical. Assess your wellness across each of these dimensions. If you feel as though you are off balance, set some specific and timely goals to obtain greater balance across each of these seven dimensions.

- Create a pie chart on how you currently are spending your time. Reflect on what you see and create a second pie chart representing how you aspire to spend your time. Now consider the actions that you need to take to move closer towards your ideal state.

Chapter 16: Be Relevant

*"As a lotus flower is born in water, grows in water and
rises out of water to stand above it unsoiled, so i,
born in the world, raised in the world,
having overcome the world, live unsoiled by the world."*

-Hindu Prince Gautama Siddharta

I thrive on building.

As a kid, I can recall building masterpieces out of Legos and building blocks. On family picnics and hiking excursions, my brothers and I would build teepees in the woods. At the beach, I could spend hours building and rebuilding sand castles with intricate moats where the water would rush in from the ocean. I built stories in my mind and captured them in my writing journals. I tore my mom's "Good Housekeeping" magazines apart building my dream home from a collage of pictures.

Throughout high school, I was always drawn to activities where I could create. Forensics (speech and debate) provided me an outlet to act out a variety of characters faced with diverse dilemmas. Student council was a creative outlet to plan and organize school dances, fundraisers, service projects and recognition activities.

In college, I was drawn to teaching because I could create lesson plans that engaged students in hands-on activities and challenged their perspectives by introducing them to new places, points of view and experiences. Through my continued commitment to service, I discovered a plethora of needs in the community, met countless nonprofits committed to advancing their missions, and realized that I could create solutions that literally changed people's lives.

In my career, I have built a nonprofit organization from the ground up, reinvented struggling nonprofits, created policy changes to drive scalable solutions, and facilitated the investment of corporate philanthropy to build communities in partnership with schools and nonprofit organizations. Through my consulting and speaking engagements, I have created and curated experiences for clients and participants that spark inspiration, foster collaboration, and deliver results.

With countless hours dedicated to building and creating over my lifetime, I have honed in on the skill of creating as a key success measure. I have accepted Thomas Edison's challenge, "There's a way to do it better – find it." **Through innovation, you differentiate yourself in a world full of people trying so hard to fit in. You attract people's attention and foster a competitive dynamic that seeks to change the world by driving greater efficiencies, more meaningful experiences, and solutions to the world's problems.**

During a leadership class that I took in high school, our teacher, Mr. Meyer, tested our creativity and our commitment to innovation by having us brainstorm 24 ways that we could make a difference in our community. What he predicted came true as I opened my notebook and went to work. The first 10-12 ideas flowed easily and related to actions that I was familiar with or had already completed. The next 5-7 ideas were harder to brainstorm and surfaced by reflecting deeper on what I had seen others in the community advance. The final set of ideas was a real struggle to identify. However, the final set of ideas was the best of the best, the top ideas reflecting "out of the box" thinking. This brainstorming exercise was an incredibly valuable tool that I continue to employ today.

The bottom line is that creative and innovative solutions are often buried deep below the surface. To uncover them, we must commit the time, remain focused and challenge our minds to connect and evolve ideas over and over again.

Think about the creative process that PR and marketing agencies go through to deliver campaigns for clients. After gathering a lot of data and context, a creative team comprised of graphic designers and artists, copywriters, editors, web designers and creative directors works on generating dozens of ideas. They capture all of their brainstorming on white boards, flip charts, and index cards. Categorizing the ideas listed into themes helps narrow the ideas, and prioritizing the themes identifies the top concepts aligned with the client's expectations, targeted deliverables, and the overall campaign vision.

In our personal and professional lives, how often do we just settle for the familiar, that which we have always done? When deciding where to eat dinner, we resort to the restaurant that we ate at a hundred times and order the same meal each time. When planning an employee recognition event at work, we repeat what was done last year. We read the same book every night to our kids or run the same trail every morning. Over time, the familiar has a tendency to become boring and lose its appeal, inspiration and source of energy. You can witness this unfold in your own behavior and attitude as well as in those engaged with you. Everyone grows less interested; participation waivers and satisfaction drops.

I do this exercise with my staff and in my workshops where I have everyone write down a solution to a problem that we are tackling. Then I ask them to pass their solutions clockwise around the room, inviting each team member to add one additional thought to each solution that passes by them. This exercise fosters a strong team culture and surfaces powerhouse ideas cultivated through a collective thinking process. The synergy of the group skyrockets as team members explain their notations and everyone's commitment to advancing innovative solutions is unwavering.

As a creator, you seek to evolve from experiences and deliver innovative options that peak people's interest. You build on the past while creating a new path. Robert Frost shares, "Two roads diverged in a wood, and I took the one less traveled by and that has made all the difference." By striking out on a path less traveled, you reignite a fire in your belly that is contagious.

So when you find yourself in a creative funk, hit the pause button on life and pull out a notebook. Free flow ideas for regaining your creative energy. Don't stop at 10-12 ideas. Push on and commit yourself to generating at least 24 ideas. Create. Evolve. Whatever you do, don't judge what is flowing from your mind but capture it before it escapes.

If you find yourself still hitting a roadblock, revert back to your childhood. Go buy some Legos or building blocks. Tinker around with them and just build. Pull out a coloring book and crayons; make yourself some refrigerator art. Visit a local art museum. Get your hands dirty at a pottery studio.

Losing yourself in a creative outlet can retrigger the flow of creative juices and get you back on track to differentiate yourself through your ideas and contributions. Challenge your ideas to evolve over time by producing multiple ideas. I believe that one of life's worst circumstances is when we believe that there is only one idea or one solution to problems that surface at home or work.

Successful individuals, companies, schools, and organizations succeed when they reflect on the words of Robert Kennedy, "There are those who look at things the way they are and ask why...I dream of things that never were and ask why not." **By dreaming of things that are not, we push ourselves to innovate, to build.** We generate solutions to the world's problems and expand the boundaries of our own minds. Our own evolution and willingness to stand out inspires others to get in the creative game and innovate.

Create and thrive!

Take Action: Be Relevant

- Take the "brainstorm 24" challenge. Think about something personally or professionally that you are trying to solve. Grab a piece of scrap paper, start brainstorming, and push through until you reach at least 24 solutions. You will see how the most creative thinking is often generated towards the later part of your brainstormed list of solutions.

- With your family, a group of friends or a team of co-workers, practice some round robin collective thinking. You can work on designing an ideal (and realistic) vacation, a community service project or a business solution. Regardless of the topic, you will find great synergy surfaces from a collective brainstorming session where everyone has the chance to build on other's ideas.

- It's creative play time. Head to your local children's museum, science center, art studio or community kitchen. Get hands on and allow your mind to embrace the experience with the curiosity of a child. Through your creative play, seek adventure and try to not hold yourself back even when you may feel awkward or uncomfortable. Leverage creative activities to draw energy, work your problem solving muscles, and step outside of your "norm."

Chapter 17: Never Stop Discovering

*"When it's time to die, let us not discover
that we have never lived."*

-Henry David Thoreau

Have you ever watched a young child explore a new toy for the first time? He examines it from every angle. He tests each button to see what it does, repeating the same actions over and over again to confirm that nothing will change. Sometimes he hands the toy to someone close by in search of additional features or for guidance on what else he can do with the toy. There is this sense of discovery that unfolds before our eyes, fueled by the child's intent to learn. He seeks to understand the toy, to engage with it, and to be entertained.

A similar discovery can unfold when reading a book to a child. She listens intently, losing herself in the pictures and hanging on each word you read. She anxiously anticipates discovering what is on the next page, sometimes not having the patience to wait until you have read every word. And then there is that moment at the end of the book when she looks at you, smiles and says, "again," as if she wants to discover the characters, storyline and ending all over again.

Children's museums and science centers can be great discovery zones, places where youth and adults alike can be hands on. The exhibits are designed to engage multiple senses, to capture and hold our attention, and to test our assumptions. Books and great storytellers can be just as engaging as museum exhibits. Animated storytellers can call our imagination into action with their captivating voices, energized body language, and colorful illustrations. We can lose track of time while fully immersed in discovery mode.

Think about the habit (or sometimes game) that many kids have of asking "why" over and over again. They hear somebody say something or read something that compels them to want to learn more, to understand why. The story of Craig Kielburger is one powerful example of how a commitment to discovering more about a particular issue can shape the course of one's life and the lives of others.

When Craig was 12, he was searching for the comics in the *Toronto Star* when he stumbled upon the story of Iqbal Masih in an article titled, "Battled Child Labour, Boy, 12, Murdered!" Iqbal was sold into slavery at the age of 4; spent most of his life chained to a carpet-weaving loom, and was killed at the age of 12 after speaking out for children's rights. Having never heard of child labor, Craig immersed himself in research including a trip to South Asia to witness poverty and child labor firsthand. He enlisted the support of his classmates to write letters, make phone calls and organize fundraisers. He leveraged speaking opportunities to increase awareness. Despite many adults not believing in the power and influence of youth, Craig launched "Free the Children" to battle child labor and poverty around the globe. His quest to discover a solution has mobilized the support of Fortune 500 companies, world leaders and celebrities like Oprah to now work in 45 countries building more than 650 schools and school rooms that provide a safe place for 55,000 children to learn each day.

Not every discovery we make is going to compel us to launch nonprofit organizations or spark some significant change in our lives or the lives of others. We will tuck most discoveries away in our minds, saving them until their relevance is revealed in a problem that we are trying to solve, advice that we are sharing or a persuasive case that we are building. What is important to keep in mind is that discoveries surface in both expected and unexpected ways. Sometimes we actively go searching for a discovery while in other cases we stumble upon one.

I have noticed that the childhood eagerness to discover new information diminishes over time. Somehow we lose our sense of exploration and adventure as we settle into our routines and points of view. Perhaps we desensitize ourselves to news that was once shocking or unimaginable, that served as the spark which compelled us to dig deeper, to learn more, or to take action. With more life experiences under our belt, our active listening skills weaken as we grow more into an autobiographical listener, someone who hears others' words and associates them with their own experiences instead of considering the speaker's context.

Often in our professional lives we become accustomed to attending the same conferences and seminars year over year, frequently complaining that the content is stale and that the presentations are stagnant. The irony is that sometimes *we* can become stagnant when we do not proactively seek out new learning opportunities, professional networks, or experiences that energize us and keep us engaged in the field's latest developments.

I have learned that it is important to balance the roles we take on in professional development throughout our careers. Sometimes we need to participate and listen to learn new content or strategies while in other cases we need to teach and pass along the lessons, observations and results that we have acquired. In the role of teacher, our assumptions and logic can be tested by the questions posed by the participants. Those questions can push us to answering the "why" behind our decisions and actions.

Think about the last time you learned something new. Where were you? What were you doing? Who were you with? How did you uncover your new discovery? Perhaps you were attending a professional development workshop with colleagues from your team at work when you discovered similarities between your team's culture and the culture described in a case study shared by the facilitator. Or maybe you were sitting at church one weekend when the pastor's message resonated with a personal struggle that you are coping with currently. Maybe a friend emailed you an article with some powerful advice that you have been searching for. You may have been at a volunteer project when you discovered more details concerning a particular social issue that you found appalling, and it challenged you to take further action. Perhaps your child may have asked you a question that you did not know the answer to for a school assignment, which led the two of you to research the answer together.

Discoveries can unfold in a variety of places. From conferences to seminars, training workshops to counseling sessions, coffee chats to books on tape, discoveries surface in both experiences and relationships. French author Andre Gide writes, **"Man cannot discover new oceans unless he has the courage to lose sight of the shore."** One

of the keys to discovery is to let go of our preconceived notions and challenge our assumptions. We have to transport ourselves outside of our current frame of reference and be willing to embark on an adventure into unchartered territory. Instead of listening and trying to associate what you hear with your **own** life experiences and relationships, try to listen to the words being spoken from the **speaker's** perspective. The "shore" in Gide's words is an analogy for our safe space, our comfort zones, and our existing frame of reference. Set yourself out to sea, far enough away from your shore, that your lack of comfort is the catalyst for greater inquiry.

When you expand your mind, life experiences, and relationships from that which is ordinary to you, you will encounter some extraordinary discoveries. It is in those moments of vulnerability that you will relive the childhood wonder that you once experienced.

Nobel Prize winner Albert Szent-Gyorgyi believed that **"discovery consists in seeing what everyone else has seen and thinking what no one else has thought."** With a greater commitment to discovery, to stretching and transforming yourself through diverse experiences and relationships, your world view will expand. The lens that you look through each day will feel different and place you at the cutting edge of innovation. The richness of your opinion will make it more valuable. The connection that you make with people will be rooted in empathy and sustained by your hunger to learn, contribute and add value.

Take Action: Never Stop Discovering

- Make connections outside of your normal viewpoint. Subscribe to a magazine outside of your industry, view a diverse array of TED Talks online, and read some biographies of leaders representing business, nonprofit, education and politics. When we go outside of our everyday point of view, we can discover inspiration and tweak solutions elsewhere to be applicable to the problems we are trying to solve. This practice can also differentiate us in our fields and challenge the status quo. I often find that there are more similarities across fields, industries and nations than there are differences.

- Teach and discover. You can teach Sunday school or guest lecture at a community college. You can facilitate brown bag lunches at your workplace on conferences you attended, hobbies or skills that you would like to cultivate in others. You can volunteer to lead workshops tied to your experiences, skills, and hobbies with kids at nonprofit programs or local schools. Regardless of the setting, I have always found that I diversify my perspective and challenge my assumptions through teaching.

Chapter 18: Stay in the Arena

"When you come to the end of your rope,
tie a knot and hang on."

-Franklin D. Roosevelt

Theodore Roosevelt once shared, "It is not the critic who counts; not the man who points out how the strong man stumbles, or where the doer of deeds could have done them better. The credit belongs to the man who is actually in the arena, whose face is marred by dust and sweat and blood; who strives valiantly; . . . who at best knows in the end the triumph of high achievement, and who at worst, if he fails, at least fails while daring greatly."

Over the past several years, I have been in the arena on a continued quest to discover my life's purpose and to live each day with passion. I have lost myself in some great books: Finding Your Element (Ken Robinson), How Will You Measure Your Life (Clayton Christensen), Start Something That Matters (Blake Mycoskie), Drive (Daniel Pink), and An Invisible Thread (Laura Schroff). I have spent countless hours seeking insight from TED and TEDx speakers from around the globe. Subscriptions to magazines such as SUCCESS, Inc., Fast Company and the Harvard Business Review have fueled my thinking along with academic lectures delivered through The Great Courses. I have followed the blog posts of an eclectic mix of leaders and philosophers, and I have written my own blog to reflect on the world around me and my experiences.

I have grown. I have become more attuned to my strengths, more embracing of my fears, and more open to being vulnerable. I am definitely far from perfect, and I am committed to staying in the arena to live each day as my most authentic self.

I have immersed myself in the work of Dr. Brene Brown, a research professor at the University of Houston's Graduate College of Social Work, a New York Times bestselling author, and a nationally renowned speaker whose 2010 TEDx Houston talk is one of the most watched talks on Ted.com with over 12 million views.

Dr. Brown writes, "We need our lives back. It's time to reclaim the gifts of imperfection—the courage to be real, the compassion we need to love ourselves and others, and the connection that gives true purpose and meaning to life. These are the gifts that bring love, laughter, gratitude, empathy and joy into our lives."

Dare to be your most authentic self.

Children's book author, Ian Wallace, once asked, "Why are you trying so hard to fit in when you were born to stand out?" We can spend our whole lives trying to please others by conforming to their interests and internalizing their judgments. Let's push those critiques aside and chose to live a more authentic life where we form our own thoughts, share our own opinions, and stand proudly as a unique individual. We must be willing to accept that our choices will not please everyone. Root the choices that you make in your values, and use both your head and your heart to navigate along your life journey. Learn from the wisdom and experience of others, but do not follow blindly the path that others have taken merely because it is easier. Instead, walk in the direction of *your* dreams.

Dare to explore your imagination.

Embrace the words, "what if." Challenge the status quo. Invent and create. Albert Einstein once said, "Imagination is everything. It is the preview of life's coming attractions." When others say it is impossible or discourage you from advancing a new idea, embrace their words as a challenge to live a more imaginative life. When you feel confined by the comfort of routine, break away and venture off into your imagination to consider how you may shake the world up. Seek adventures in new places with new people that deliver experiences that challenge your perspective.

Dare to reach your potential.

We lost a great world leader in 2013 when Nelson Mandela passed away. The world was inspired by his unwavering commitment to change and his long journey to fulfilling his potential. The words of William Henley inspired Mandela throughout his time in prison: "I am the master of my fate; I am the captain of my soul." Seize each day as an opportunity to learn and grow, to shape and evolve, and to challenge and celebrate. When you feel as though your potential has been met, push on and take pleasure in the surprise of how much more you have within.

Dare to inspire.

I believe that we are all joy seekers, waking each day in pursuit of something that puts a smile on our face, fills the air with laughter and gives us the feeling that we belong, that we are connected to something greater than ourselves. We each want to contribute something meaningful; we want our lives to have purpose. It is what fuels us day after day, week after week. We are drawn to those that inspire. Consider yourself a source of inspiration for others; chose your words and actions wisely. Remember that we each can create the joy that we seek and spread the compassion that we yearn for in life. When we celebrate our imperfections, it is a reminder that we are all human and interconnected with one another.

Dare to stay in the arena.

Life is hard. We each face challenges that we believe are insurmountable. Relationships have their bumps and bruises. Our work can lack inspiration which effects our motivation. Others may try holding us back in pursuit of their own gain. The internal conflicts that we grapple with each day impact our mood, actions and sense of self-worth. But we win each day that we return to the arena and stand ready to embrace whatever comes our way. We must trust in our own ability to survive, leverage the inspiration of others to stay in the game, confront our fears and accept our imperfections. If we step outside of the arena, we may never know what we are capable of achieving, our story will stand incomplete, and we will have deprived the world of the gifts we were born to share.

Let's "dare greatly" together. Let's support one another rather than knock each other down. Let's inspire more and judge less.

Benjamin Franklin once said, "All mankind is divided into three classes: those that are immovable, those that are movable, and those that move." Let's not stand in the way of our own potential or allow others to dictate our next steps. Let's move to the beat of our dreams and the rhythm of our soul with our head and heart in the game.

See you in the arena!

Take Action: Stay in the Arena

- View Dr. Brene Brown's popular TED Talk on vulnerability and explore some of her online interviews with Oprah and Jonathan Fields from the Good Life Project.

- Reflect back on some of your greatest successes and identify some of the initial fears that you had in achieving those outcomes. Consider what helped you overcome or overrule your fears. Now think about some of the goals that you are pursuing currently and some of the fears that you are facing. Often times, many of the strategies that we have used in the past to charge through our fears to success can work in present day situations that we find ourselves in.

- Identify those individuals that are in your "safety zone" where you can be 100% of yourself and completely vulnerable. Surprise those individuals with a hand-written thank you note acknowledging their friendship, support and strength.

My Closing Wish

"I believe that every right implies a responsibility,
every opportunity an obligation;
every possession a duty."

-John D. Rockefeller Jr.

Let's be crazy!

When was the last time you did something crazy? When did you last take a big, bold step away from the status quo and let your passion uncontrollably surface through your words and actions without filtering or fearing the consequences of your authenticity being on display?

It makes me sad how often we starve the world of our stories and give power to an inner voice that disregards our own potential. We let the judgments of others reproduce in our minds, suffocating our dreams and blinding us to the vision that is our purpose.

When we're crazy, we disregard it all. We bring our whole being to the table through our imagination, innovation and creation. We differentiate ourselves from one another while simultaneously celebrating our interdependence. We use criticism as fuel and rejection as motivation. Most importantly, we don't give up in the pursuit of something greater than what has been deemed possible. Instead, we pursue with great fervor the impossible as an agent of change and miracle worker.

So let's stop being safe and start being bold. Let's step out of our routines and predictable thoughts, and let's be spontaneous. Take a step off the beaten path and discover a new horizon. Let's put down the status quo, pass by the tried and true and challenge ourselves to innovate, to create something new. Bypass the fear of judgment and rejection and embrace the spirit of entrepreneurs who seek to disrupt and deliver solutions that simplify and accelerate.

Let's be crazy and different and break the rules that we have blindly embraced and never truly dissected to understand the "why" behind the words. Let's be magical in a quest to hear our naysayers erupt in a chorus of oohs and aahs.

Let's plow through the "no's" and "can'ts" and "shouldn'ts." Let's shake out the fear and change the language in our minds. And let's surround ourselves with teachers, mentors and advocates that feed us inspiration and nourish our souls so that we can thrive by embracing the rawest form of ourselves. Peel off the labels, tune out the destructive criticism and tune into our passion which breeds the stories that only we can create and share.

Let's...be...crazy!

ABOUT THE AUTHOR

Daniel is a curator of inspiration. He seeks to change the world by equipping, elevating and evolving others through his words and actions. Daniel is an avid student of life, striving to learn from each person he encounters and each experience that he embraces.

For more information on Daniel,
check out his website at www.dghorgangroup.com.